The Perfect Prayer

The Perfect Prayer

Unleash the Power of Prayer to Revolutionize Your Life

Jeff Daws

with Joe Oliver

XULON PRESS

Xulon Press
2301 Lucien Way #415
Maitland, FL 32751
407.339.4217
www.xulonpress.com

CONTENTS

Dedication

I dedicate this book to my life-long mentor, spiritual father, and friend, Reverend Jerry Chitwood. Brother Chitwood, you saw in me more than I ever saw in myself. You took a chance on me when no one else would by giving me my first opportunity to serve God's Kingdom full time at a church as your youth pastor. Over 30 years have come and gone from our first meeting, and you have never stopped believing in me or encouraging me. You have taught me to love God's Word more than just preaching it. Your influence in my life has made me a better leader, pastor, father, and husband. God has used you to make me a better man. Thank you for always being available for me no matter what hour I called. I dedicate this book to you because you have allowed me to stand on your shoulders to do more for Jesus. I am forever grateful for your investment in me.

Acknowledgments

I want to thank Emmalyn Roell, Chesnee Dorsey, Rhonda Daws, and Joe Oliver for all of their ideas and feedback as I worked on this book. I'm so grateful for their insights. They helped me take this book to the next level. And I want to say a special "thank you" to everyone mentioned in this book who was willing to share their story of challenge, setback, and ultimate victory. My prayer is that many lives will be touched and changed by their testimony that God always has the final say in everything.

Chapter 1

When All Looked Lost

The year was 2003, and I sat weeping at my office desk. Despite trying everything I knew about growing a church, ours was falling apart around me. My assistant, Angie Benton, had just informed me that within days, we had to make a mortgage payment and that we didn't have enough money in our account to pay it or the staff salaries. My vision of a vibrant, growing church in Stockbridge, Georgia, was dying before my eyes, and I didn't know what to do.

Having exhausted every idea I had of how to rescue our sinking ship, I concluded that it was all over. The church had failed...*I had failed*. Misery gripped my stomach as I envisioned myself getting up in front of the congregation that following Sunday and having to share with them the undeniable truth that our church would have to close its doors.

I couldn't see any way out. I couldn't think of any way to reverse the situation. I was out of ideas and out of time. I was defeated.

Where was God?

I bowed my head and cried. How had it come to this?

A few years before, our church had been meeting in a small building in Rex, Georgia. We were out of room and had no place to build. So I spent much time in prayer and believed that God was leading us to a new location. We started a building program to raise money for the move, found a tract of property that we could develop, and began the long, hard process of building a new facility.

I thought building our new church would be fairly simple. All we had to do was get permits, clear the land, construct the church, and put in a parking lot. Well, it was anything but simple! It seemed that every day, new problems appeared from every direction, and most of them cost much more money than I had thought.

Finally, after two years of meeting in a school to keep the congregation together and after many, many sleepless nights concerned about whether we would even be successful in completing the new building, we opened our new church facility in Stockbridge.

And I was relieved, because in the back of my mind, I had kept telling myself that everything would be fine once we got into the new building. In fact, many times during the building program, I kept myself encouraged and pushed through overwhelming exhaustion with the belief that better times were right around the corner. But to my shock, the situation worsened.

Almost as soon as we opened the new building, a disgruntled group in my congregation broke away, taking about a third of the church's giving with them. What hurt the most about this was that these were good people who I had known for years. I had prayed over them, visited when they were sick, baptized them and their family members, called them to check on them, and much, much more. I considered some of them to be very close friends. And just when I thought they might choose to be a part of my vision for reaching our community for God, they left.

As if things couldn't get any worse, the atmosphere in our first deacon meeting in the new building was odd. Instead of celebrating the accomplishment of completing the new building in spite of the countless challenges, the deacons just stared at me as I shared my vision for our church. After returning home, a late-night phone call revealed why I had been given such a cold shoulder. The deacons had decided it was time for me to step down as pastor of the church.

Words cannot describe how shocked, angry, and devastated I was after hearing this. I felt completely gutted, like my friends had backstabbed me at the very moment we were entering into a new world of ministry possibilities and hope!

"How could this get any worse?!" I groaned as I realized that I'd have to confront each of these gentlemen, some of whom I'd known for many years, and try to resolve this mess.

Throughout all of this, I remained faithful in my daily prayer and Bible reading time. In fact, I truly believe that the reason I'm still alive and able to talk to you today through this book is because God heard my prayers and kept me sane. I believe that God can do the miraculous and that he is a God that gives breakthroughs!

And yet, that fateful day in 2003 came anyway.

———

I sat at my desk and lifted the paper bank statement Angie had given me. I knew that our church's finances were low. After the dissenters left, giving and attendance sharply declined. Instead of our church snowballing into greater and greater things, we were going backwards and fast! We were in a financial avalanche, and I had no way of stopping it.

The bank statement showed a balance of $8,000, but our mortgage payment due that week was $8,200. I felt so sick in my stomach. I knew that we weren't going to be able to pay any of our staff. I shook my head not knowing how I would be able to look them in the eyes and tell them we wouldn't be able to pay them.

It was over, all over.

I collapsed onto my desk in tearful prayer. I cried out to God, "I'm so sorry that I've let you and these people down! I've failed as a pastor and a leader. It isn't your fault; it's my fault. I'll tell your people that I've failed and that we'll sell this building and disband. I don't know what else to do, God! I'll resign from being a pastor. I'll go to another church and tithe there. I'll be a good Christian. I'm so sorry I've failed you!"

Suddenly, my office phone rang. I could see that Angie was calling. I tried to calm myself and lifted the phone.

"Hey, pastor," she said, "there's a group of men here who want to look at our building."

I thanked her and hung up. I took a long, deep breath, rubbed my eyes with tissues, and swallowed. "So, this is the end, God," I thought, thinking about the prayer I had just prayed. "That was quick." I rose from my desk and walked out of my office with as much salesman confidence as I could muster.

You Want to Do What?!

Obviously, the men had stopped by to take a tour of our facility, so I was going to give them one that showcased our building. Greeting the three men cheerfully, I immediately turned and escorted them out of the front office and into the auditorium. I flipped on the bright lights in the large room and began walking down the aisle. I slowed as they hesitated to go any further in the room, their puzzled faces telling me that something was wrong.

"Gentlemen," I asked, "what do you think of the building?"

Bewildered, one of the three corrected, "Pastor, we love your building, but that's not what we're here to see you about."

"Oh," I choked out. I could feel the blood running out of my face as my expression changed from excitement to disappointment. "Oh. Then what can I do for you?"

One of the men replied, "Pastor...your church owns one of our churches."

I was taken aback for a moment. I was not expecting to hear those words, and I had no clue where the conversation was going. Years back, we had owner-financed our first church building to a church that wanted to expand its daycare facility. It seemed like a good idea at the time, but after only a few payments, they filed for bankruptcy. We received a letter from the court saying that we couldn't even contact these people. Worse still, our lawyer told us that we would never get our money back. As painful as it was, our church lost the property and its value.

Or so I thought.

Stepping forward, one of the men said, "I'm the bishop of my denomination, and I apologize for the way these people have treated your church. I have with me my chief financial officer." He motioned to the side. "He is going to write you a check for the remaining balance of what we owe you."

You'd think that I would jump for joy and run around the auditorium shouting praises to God after hearing such news, but I didn't because there was a catch. I shook my head in disappointed frustration.

I replied, "I'd love to sell you that building, but the borrower put the name of his church on the loan. And since he's taken off and I can't even talk to him, we can't legally sell that church building to you. It would be like me trying to sell my neighbor's house to you."

The bishop sighed, and after some more discussion placed his card in my hand. "Call me if anything changes," he said. And the three men were gone.

I walked back into the office, my head filled with conflicting thoughts. I had gone from complete defeat, to surprise, to hope, to feeling like I'd had the rug pulled out from underneath me. While I stood in silent thought, Angie swiveled in her chair and casually asked, "Can't we sell those guys the note on the old church?"

Suddenly, it was like fireworks going off in my head!

We could sell them the loan of our old church!

I ran back to my desk, picked up the phone, and hastily dialed the number on the bishop's business card. With resurrected hope in my voice, I announced over the phone, "Bishop...I can't sell you our old church building...but I CAN sell you the bank note!"

I want you to know that the week that we were going under, the week that began with absolutely no hope, no solutions, and no ideas about how to turn everything around, the week that could've marked the end of Stockbridge Community Church was the week that ended with God miraculously working through people we didn't even know to answer our cries for help. On Monday, we had $8,000 in our church's account. On Friday, we had $157,000!

I tell you this story to declare to you that it isn't over until God says it's over. As you read through this book, it is my prayer and hope to help you unlock confidence in God through the power of prayer.

Chapter 2

Pray about It

"*J*ust pray about it!" How many times have you heard that statement before? If you're a Christian, you've probably given lots of people this piece of advice along the way. Sometimes you may have said it with confidence; other times you may have said it because you had no idea what else to say to someone.

But what do those words mean to people? Are we suggesting that they pray the same prayer they pray before eating a meal like, "God is great; God is good." Are we talking about a child's bedtime prayer like, "Now I lay me down to sleep." Maybe we're talking about a prayer that sounds more like Shakespeare than modern English: "Thouest, greatest, God..."

When I was young in church, I'd hear pastors pray in very unusual ways and think that they had some kind of special connection with God that regular people didn't have. I'd observe people in my church that were considered very spiritual. I noticed that if they were asked to pray over offering or at the close of a service, they would suddenly speak like a different person. Their voice would become deeper, more resonant, and they would put great emotion into their King James words, almost like a play. I remember sitting there on the church pew, listening to them pray, thinking that sometimes it sounded very beautiful and that sometimes it sounded like a tongue twister.

How Should We Pray?

If you've been in church for any length of time, you've probably heard that you should read your Bible and pray every day—which is great advice that I've been living by for years now. But, when we get down to the nitty gritty, the brass tacks, the essential truth, *how does* one pray?

When I was a new Christian, I had no idea how to answer this question. So I started my own exploration for the answer by going around the church and asking, who I thought were the most spiritual people, how to pray. And I got some very interesting responses to my questions.

A few told me to pray the Scriptures. For instance, instead of reading John 3:16 to myself, they recommended that I open up my Bible during my prayer time and start praying out loud some verses, like this: "Dear God, 'For God so loved the world, that he gave his only begotten son...'" Needless to say, this method of prayer did not work at all for me. I felt like all I was doing was reading out loud a passage as if I were in school, standing up to read a page in a book. I didn't feel like I was pouring my heart out to God, and I definitely didn't feel like I was connecting with God and growing closer to him.

Still no closer to understanding prayer, I became excited when an upcoming "All Night Prayer Meeting" was announced in church one Sunday morning. That really got me thinking. My first thought was, "Is God up all night?" My second thought worried me quite a lot: "What in the world was I going to say to God all night long?!" I remembered the idea that I needed to pray the Scriptures, so I envisioned myself reading the Bible at the prayer meeting. With that much time, I made a bet with my teenage self that I could read the whole New Testament!

But I really wanted to know how to pray. So I signed up for the all-night meeting, and, oh boy, was I in for an education!

As the prayer meeting started that night in the church auditorium, it began rather orderly with the pastor welcoming everyone and giving a few details on how the meeting would unfold. But once he closed his eyes and began praying in a deep, commanding voice, it seemed like everyone in the room broke off to pray in a different way. Some people rushed down to pray at the altar; others knelt at the pew they had been sitting at. Still others walked around the room praying loudly. I noticed some sat very still and prayed silently, while others made vigorous motions with their arms as they prayed aloud.

I picked out the people who I thought were the most spiritual in the crowd, and by chance, they also seemed to be the loudest ones in the room. Like a light bulb going off in my brain, I concluded, "To get my prayers answered, I need to pray *loud!*" I was learning now!

I also realized that my spiritual mentors were starting to say the same things over and over. Phrases like, "I love you, Jesus," and "God, you can do it," and "Hallelujah," kept coming out of their mouths. Please understand that I'm not knocking saying these things from your heart. These phrases are an important part of worshipping and praising God. But since I was trying to learn to pray to God, I learned that night that if I wanted to get God's attention, I just needed to say the same phrases over and over in a loud voice.

And that *is* the way I prayed for *years!*

Then, I married Rhonda.

Could You Tone It Down?

We moved into a small duplex. At first, I didn't care who heard me pray or how loud I prayed. After all, I wanted God to hear me, and in order for that to happen, I had to pray loud and with great forcefulness to storm the heavenlies! One morning, Rhonda cautiously approached me and gently asked if I could pray a little quieter. She said she was afraid that the neighbors would hear all of the noise and mistake my rafter-rattling prayers for a domestic dispute!

I'd like to say that I welcomed her suggestion, but at first, I was quite sore that she would even insinuate that I needed to tone down my prayers. I mean, didn't she realize that I was praying to God?

But this got me thinking. Maybe loud, repetitive prayers were not the answer to connecting with God. Maybe—just maybe, the spiritual giants at my old church had missed something in their attempts to commune with the Creator. And if they had missed something, I had missed something in copying their behavior.

I realized that I needed to find a better way to pray.

Journal It!

Not too long after Rhonda and mine's disagreement about how loud I should pray, I heard a speaker describing how to pray by writing out prayers. Instantly, I thought, "Hey, Rhonda would like that!"

I began writing in a prayer journal using the **ACTS** model of prayer.

Adoration: Give God praise and honor for who he is

Confession: Honestly deal with sin in your life

Thanksgiving: Say what you're grateful for in your life

Supplication: Pray for the needs of others and yourself

Suddenly through my prayer journal, I found a way to speak differently to God than I ever had. Instead of repeating the same things over and over to God, I found new ways to express my gratitude toward him and deeper insights into what was going on in my life.

Writing down my prayers was an enormous step for me (I didn't really like to write at the time). But it produced positive, visible fruit in my spiritual life.

If you're new to prayer or find yourself saying the same old things to God every time you pray, I recommend prayer journaling to get you started in exploring a whole new world of communication with God. Couple it with the ACTS method, and you've got a very powerful set of tools to get you praying stronger.

But what if I told you that there was an even better way to pray?

The Perfect Prayer?

After writing my prayers down for a few years and using **ACTS**, I began wondering if there was still a better way to pray.

During this time, I had joined a coaching class for pastors designed to help them improve and grow in every aspect of leadership and ministry. On this particular day, while I sat waiting for the next session of instruction to begin, I noticed the name Dr. Elmer L. Towns next to the topic of prayer on the speaker schedule.

At this point, I was a bit skeptical that anyone could teach me more about prayer than what I already had learned...*but* I was also a bit curious. If there was a better way to pray, then I wanted to learn it and use it!

A quick introduction to the audience was made, and with noticeable interest from all the pastors in the room, an older gentleman shuffled to the lectern. With a keen voice and a point of his finger, he proclaimed to the assembly, "I pray the perfect prayer every day. Would you like to know how to do it?"

I almost fell out of my chair.

"The perfect prayer?"

Here was the very thing that I wanted to know!

I leaned forward, with my pen ready to fill up my notebook with every important detail that he'd reveal. But before he shared his secret with the group, he told us about where his life's journey with God had taken him.

After attending an evangelistic meeting at the age of 18, Towns decided that he wanted to commit his whole life to serving God. By age 19, he was pastoring a church that had previously closed in Savannah, Georgia. He dug deep into Christian studies in college and was extremely interested in discovering the factors that caused churches to grow.

Along the way, he eventually served with Jerry Falwell at Thomas Road Baptist Church, the 9th largest church in America at the time. Towns related to us how Falwell felt that God wanted them to build a college that would raise up a generation of Christians who were both educated and passionate about serving God. Together, he and Falwell founded what would become Liberty University.

So you might think that just because God was behind the founding of this college that everything went smoothly and that every problem was miraculously swept away at first notice. In reality, tremendous challenges almost immediately exploded!

Dr. Towns shared with us that the college ran into huge financial difficulties—after all, paying for large buildings and staff salaries and maintenance and a multitude of other random expenses related to running a college does not come cheap! Worse still, the college was built on the Thomas Road Baptist Church's property, so if it went under, the church would lose its WHOLE campus!

Wow! Talk about a migraine-inducing, oh-my-God-how-do-we-fix-this dilemma!

So what did Falwell do as his God-inspired dream came crashing down in flames? Towns says that Falwell fasted and prayed and prayed and fasted.

Even as Falwell met with bankers and lawyers and businessmen and every door of possible help slammed shut in his face, Falwell continued to pray. But the stress was taking its toll on him. Dr. Towns noticed that his friend's body was showing the ragged signs of unending pressure. Nevertheless, according to Towns, Falwell refused to give up and refused to let go of God.

Then out of the blue, when all hope looked lost, a businessman phoned Falwell. He had just seen the preacher on TV and felt compelled to help him turn around the dreadful financial situation at the school. God does answer prayer!

Today, Liberty University is one of the largest Christian universities in the world. Including their online courses, this school has over a 100,000 enrolled each year! The university itself is a combination of 17 colleges, including a school of law and a school of medicine, with over 600 areas of study! All of this almost never happened. But through the power of prayer, God transformed the calamity into abundant prosperity!

Even when it seems like God is doing nothing behind the scenes, my friend, I can assure you that God IS doing SOMETHING. I can't stress to you enough how important it is for you to turn to God in prayer with everything that is important to you.

But what is the perfect prayer, according to Dr. Towns?

Chapter 3

Why Pray?

As I sat in the classroom, surrounded by other pastors on the edge of their seats, listening to Dr. Elmer Towns describe event after event in his life where God had moved miraculously on his behalf, I wondered what this man's great prayer secret was. I visualized myself being able to have a direct connection with God. Being candid, it wasn't that I wanted this type of access to God's throne room just to spend time with him. I confess to you that, at that time in my life, all I wanted was for my prayers to be answered, and in my mind, if there was a way to jump to the front of the line with my requests, I wanted to know how to do it.

I fidgeted in my seat, wanting Dr. Towns to just cut to the chase and reveal his secret.

Dr. Towns seemed to notice a growing eagerness from his audience, paused, but instead of jumping to what everyone in the room wanted him to say, pivoted his conversation to his supreme focus.

"JESUS," he emphasized. "He was known as a great person of faith and prayer. People would walk for miles just to see him. Just to be around him..."

Origin of Jesus' Power

I envision Jesus walking dusty roads, encircled by a crowd wherever he went. Like Mother Teresa, his heart went out to the poor and sick. Like Billy Graham, he longed to shine the light of God's truth into the darkness of the world.

I've always found it fascinating that even though Jesus is the son of God, he took the time to pray daily. Mark 1:35 says, "Very early in the morning, while it was still dark, Jesus got up, left the house and went off to a solitary place, where he prayed."

The crowds of people came and listened to him. Mark 6:34 records that "When Jesus landed and saw a large crowd, he had compassion on them...and he began teaching them many things." According to Mark 1:22, "The people were amazed at his teaching, because he taught them as one who had authority."

And what about Jesus' ability to perform miracles? The Gospels are filled with miracles that Jesus granted. Among the many written down, he healed the lame so that they could walk again, restored mute people the ability to speak, and fed multitudes with a child's basket of fish and bread.

John chapter 9 describes one of these extraordinary miracles. Jesus and his disciples encountered a man who had been blind from birth. Jesus' disciples asked Jesus whether the blind man was being punished by God for his personal sins or for those of his parents. Jesus astounded his disciples by declaring that the blind man wasn't being punished by God at all but was blind so that God could demonstrate his healing power to the world.

And in the presence of many witnesses, Jesus spit on the ground, made some mud, and put it on the blind man's eyes. That may sound disgusting to you—it does to me—but once the blind man washed off the muck in the Pool of Siloam, he could see clearly!

This same miracle-working Jesus, through whom such power flowed, didn't just do these things on his own. The Bible records over and over again that Jesus took the time to PRAY *before* he ministered to people and *during* his ministry with people.

The disciples were perplexed by how God could use one person to do so many miraculous and supernatural things. Finally, as recorded in Luke 11:1, one of them got up enough nerve to say, "Lord, teach us to pray."

In my mind, I imagine Jesus smiling at this disciple and thinking with a chuckle, "*Finally*, someone asks me!" That's just my own take, but the disciples of Jesus, the ones who observed his actions and heard his words day and night, knew that he was very, very different from anyone that they had ever encountered.

He wasn't like the religious leaders, quarreling over rules and interpretations of the Law. He wasn't like so many of the wealthy and the tax collectors, who ignored the poor or made their lives even more miserable than they already were. He wasn't like kings, who pretended to be like gods, untouchable, unknowable, uncaring. He wasn't like rebel leaders, who stirred up the crowds to try to overthrow the government with swords and knives.

Jesus walked in the powerful yet peace-bringing presence of God and poured out compassion and healing for the broken and sick. And at the core of Jesus' unrivaled external power and tranquil internal peace was his daily commitment to prayer. *Prayer!*

Prayer makes the difference!

Are you ready to learn how to deepen and strengthen your prayers?

Chapter 4

How to Pray

*H*aving just asked Jesus how to pray, one of the disciples eagerly awaited Jesus' answer. Perhaps he thought it was going to be a magic formula or the right combination of words like: "One, two, three, let it be! Four, five, six, do it quick! Seven, eight, nine, do it this time!" I'm joking here.

That phrase sounds absolutely ridiculous, but you know that if it worked, people would say it! If you look at every religion that has ever existed throughout history, you'd find countless similarly ridiculous rituals and "magical" phrases that have been used by people trying to get some supernatural power out in the universe to help them. Jesus, on the other hand, knew how to directly communicate with God and cut through all of the chaotic ways that people were trying to get God's attention.

Interestingly, Jesus began his teaching on prayer by warning us about how NOT to pray! Take a look at Matthew 6:5-8:

> "When you pray, don't be like the hypocrites who love
> to pray publicly on street corners and in the synagogues

where everyone can see them...But when you pray, go away by yourself, shut the door behind you, and pray to your Father in private. Then your Father, who sees everything, will reward you. When you pray, don't babble on and on as people of other religions do. They think their prayers are answered merely by repeating their words again and again. Don't be like them, for your Father knows exactly what you need even before you ask him."

Whenever Jesus says "DON'T", you know it's extremely important! First, he cautions us not to pray like a hypocrite publicly, saying all kinds of things to impress the people listening as opposed to speaking from an honest heart to God the Father. During Jesus' time, religious leaders in the Jewish faith would pray loudly on street corners, in the synagogues, and at the temple to proudly demonstrate to everyone how spiritual they were. (Kind of reminds me of that prayer meeting I went to as a teenager.) Jesus, being all about truth and genuineness, called these people out for the mismatch between their public piety and their private sinfulness.

Second, Jesus instructs us not to *babble* or say the same things over and over. In Jesus' day—as well as before and even still today—people repeated short phrases to themselves throughout the day as a magical charm to ward off evil and bring them good luck. Jesus blatantly says this is *not* how we should pray.

So How Should We Pray?

1. We should pray *honestly*.

Prayer should be honest communication with God. We learn from Jesus that God isn't looking for the most elaborate ritual and wording that can be conceived by human ingenuity. God is looking at our hearts for honesty: the good, the bad, and the ugly. He really doesn't care about flowery, Shakespearean wording; he's interested in us sharing with him from our hearts!

To Be Like...

When I became a pastor, one of my primary tasks was to preach. So, I started listening to how other preachers preached and prayed, and I tried to copy them. One pastor on TV, John Hagee, was a *manuscript preacher*—meaning that he wrote out his entire sermon, word for word, and then delivered it by teleprompter like when politicians make televised speeches. I'm not criticizing this style of public speaking; in fact, it worked great for John Hagee!

But when I tried out this style, it was a complete flop. I kept looking down at my notes, ignoring the audience, but then would look up, trying to make eye contact with the people in the room, just to look back down at my notes and realize that I was lost in the sea of words! This style just wasn't me.

So I moved on and tried to be like the very successful and well-known Atlanta pastor Dr. Paul Walker. This brilliant man never used notes and could quote over 20 Bible verses in every sermon. Sometimes he would quote verses perfectly, word-for-word, in rapid fire. *Bam! Bam! Bam!* When I tried to copy his method, I would get all tongue-tied trying to quickly quote Scripture, and the end result was always a train wreck. *BAM!* And I'd get details all mixed up. I'd put Moses in the ark, Noah parting the Red Sea, and Jesus in the belly of the whale! *BAM!*

Looking for a new model, my TV channel landed on a famously dynamic preacher named T. D. Jakes. He peppered his sermons with catchy word pictures like, "Ladies, God is going to get so close to you, he is going to get between you and your make up!" I loved his witty sayings; his crowd loved his sayings; so I thought I'd create some of my own to spice up my messages. There was only one problem: I was horrible at this! I tried my own variation of the one above and it came out as, "Men, God is going to get closer to you than your deodorant!" I smiled at the audience waiting for their reaction, but most people just stared back either confused or unimpressed. Fail!

Finally, I came across a pastor of a megachurch on the West Coast named Rick Warren, who counsels to just be yourself. I thought about that for a long time. "Just be yourself." I wondered if people would like me for who I was. But there was only one way to find out.

To my surprise, when I stopped trying to be like other people and just presented myself to people as I am, faults and all, I started really connecting with my audience. And I no longer felt like a hypocrite, trying to pretend to be some big shot TV preacher, which I just royally goofed up anyway.

"So, how does all of that relate to prayer?" you might ask. Well, my friend, here's how it relates to prayer: When you pray, don't pray like a hypocrite. Like the ones that Jesus pointed out, who prayed loudly in public, hypocrites are only concerned about looking good in front of other people and in trying to impress them. As recorded in Matthew 23:27, Jesus even went as far as to call them painted tombs: They look great outside, but inside are filled with rotting bones!

God isn't impressed with fancy words. And if you're praying out loud with people, you shouldn't try to impress them with your words either. Instead, be yourself. Speak to God as you normally would speak every day. God is really, really, REALLY interested in your heart.

Pray honestly! Honestly, pray!

Miracle on a Construction Site

I have a friend named Tim who struggled with alcohol. He shared with me about how he would pray to God, over and over, prayers like "God, please help me," and "God do you love me?" and "God, I need your help because I can't seem to help myself."

Complicating matters, Tim worked as a heavy equipment operator—a job where being drunk while working could cause expensive damage to property, personal injury, or even death.

One morning, Tim was climbing up onto the bulldozer when he felt like he just couldn't take it anymore. So, he prayed an honest prayer, perhaps the most honest one in his life. He shared with me his short but gut-wrenchingly honest prayer: "God, I need you because this alcohol is destroying me and my family. Help me, God. Please, help me!" He looked up at the sky, expecting a reply, but nothing came.

Shrugging his shoulders, Tim started up the bulldozer and started clearing land. Suddenly, he caught sight of a white truck, with "County Inspector" painted on the side, slowly driving by his dig site. A chill went down Tim's spine as he realized that the company he worked for hadn't posted any permits on the premises. Without properly posted permits, the project could be fined or shut down, and for Tim, that would mean no paychecks to support his family.

When Tim reported the situation to his employer, the employer didn't seem that interested, casually remarking on the phone that he had the permits and that someone would come out and put it up sometime. Now, Tim was nervous, because if the county inspector came by again and no permit was displayed, Tim would have to be the one to talk to him. Feeling the pressure, Tim licked his lips. "It'd be a great time for a drink," he thought. But he remembered his prayer earlier in the day and pushed the idea out of his mind.

Another day dawned, and Tim was once again driving the bulldozer across the work site, when, out of the corner of his eye, he saw the same white truck trolling along the road by the property. The permits were still not posted! He felt sick in the stomach, wondering when someone from his company was going to do their job, get out there, and put up a few pieces of paper! Tim breathed a sigh of relief as the white truck abruptly accelerated and disappeared from view.

The sun moved across the sky, and still no one from the company showed up to post the permits. And then it happened! The white truck appeared once again, slowed, and pulled into the dusty worksite. Trundling along the uneven ground, it pulled right up to Tim's bulldozer and parked.

Tim swallowed hard as the truck door opened and a man stepped out. Tim's heart sank; the man did not look happy.

Turning off the rumbling bulldozer, Tim climbed down and wondered how he was going to pay his bills once the inspector shut them down. Tim started to speak, but the inspector cut him off loudly.

"You're' the one I've been looking for!"

Puzzled, Tim was about to explain that he was not the company or property owner, when the inspector directly announced, "You're the man with an alcohol problem who's been asking God for help!"

Tim reeled in shock. His mouth dropped open. He was speechless! Who was this guy? How did he know what he had been praying?!

His face now showing compassion, the inspector revealed, "Sir, I've been driving around the past few days looking for you because God told me that there was a man out here who was struggling with alcohol who needed my help."

Feeling wobbly in his knees, Tim nodded. Tears formed in his eyes, and he confessed, "It's me...Yep, it's me. You found me."

From that moment, the inspector helped Tim begin his road to recovery from alcoholism. The two formed a strong bond of friendship, and the inspector introduced Tim to a recovery group at his church.

At the writing of this book, Tim has been free from the grip of alcoholism for 15 years! And he traces it all back to one morning when he prayed an honest prayer to God for help.

What about you? Is there something that you'd like to openly share with God that you need help with? I encourage you to stop reading, bow your head, and tell God what you need. What do you have to lose? Or better, what do you have to gain?

2. We should pray *continually*.

Back in Matthew 6:7, Jesus warned us not to babble the same words over and over as if we were pagans. But in 1 Thessalonians 5:16-17, Paul instructs us to "Be joyful always; pray continually." Is it even humanly possible to pray continually?

For years, I felt like my prayer time was too short. As a new Christian, I thought that I was supposed to pray for an hour each day. But, like I heard in that all-night prayer meeting at my church, my spiritual mentors at the time repeated a lot of the same words and phrases in their prayers. So when I prayed—especially if I was trying to pray for a full hour—I found myself repeating the same things to fill up my hour of prayer.

Somewhere along the way while I was praying, I suddenly stopped and asked myself, "Jeff, is your heart in this?" Was my heart, my motives, my emotions, my mind fully behind the words coming out of my mouth in prayer to God, or was I merely saying a mantra, a chant, a bunch of religious-sounding but meaningless words to me? This was a powerful turning point in thought for me, and it can be for you as well.

Since Jesus revealed that God the Father doesn't want us to pray meaningless repetitions of words to him, how in the world can we pray *continually* throughout our day. Part of the answer is in how we define *continually*, but before I get to that, let me stir up a memory from your past or present.

Do you remember being in school and hearing from a teacher that there was going to be a huge test at the end of the week? You might be in school right now and are experiencing the flood of anxiety that so many test takers feel. It's been over three decades since I've been in school, and yet a shudder still sweeps over me when I think about having to take any kind of test.

Even before I was a Christian, you better believe that I prayed days before the exam that I'd pass, on the day of the test that I'd pass, while taking it that I'd pass, and the next day that somehow, I'd passed! You may have just chuckled or squirmed remembering similar experiences from when you were in school.

Here's my point: I believe that continual prayer in the Christian life isn't literally being on your knees praying to God 24 hours a day, 7 days a week. I believe that it is a daily communing with God—a state of being where we are aware that God is with us and at any time, we can turn to him, out loud or in our mind, and have an honest conversation with him about anything.

Thinking about continual prayer in this way suddenly frees prayer from being limited to just a few words in the morning or before meals or before going to sleep. Suddenly, prayer becomes instantly available to us ANY TIME.

As a pastor, many times people will come to me to share about a crisis that is tearing them and their family apart. While I listen to them, I will silently ask God, "What would you like me to say to this person?"

I believe that God is always present with us, wherever we are, whatever the time and circumstances. So why not just turn to him in conversation as we go through our day and invite him into our decisions, our concerns, our celebrations, our wonder at the world around us, our needs, our sorrows, our joy—every part of our human life?

To me, this is what continual prayer means, and I encourage you to begin inviting God into your day. If you see a beautiful sunset, turn to God and tell him how much you marvel at his creation. If you see an ambulance speed by, pause a moment in your mind to ask God to help those who are in need of medical assistance and the health workers that are caring for them. If you hear of a friend or coworker or family member that is experiencing something bad, pause and pray for them. If you get an unexpected blessing, immediately say thank you to God!

God takes delight in our lives, so continually share your life with him.

3. We should pray with *expectation*.

Did you know that Jesus made a specific promise about prayer? And let me tell you, when Jesus makes a promise, you can build your whole life on it!

So what is this amazing promise about prayer? Jesus made it in Matthew 6:6, where he said the following:

"When you pray, go into your room, close the door, and pray to your Father, who is unseen. Then your Father, who sees what is done in secret, will reward you."

A lot of times, we read over verses quickly or don't take note of things that may seem unimportant or obvious to us, but pause and take a moment to consider that IF you pray, God WILL reward you.

Many people think of prayer as a drudgery, something that just has to be done if you're a Christian. It's *give, give, give* to God with nothing received in return. But according to Jesus, that statement is not true at all. If we pray honestly and continually, we should EXPECT God to respond.

The Cattle on a Thousand Hills

In 1924, Dallas Theological Seminary was founded but almost immediately ran into dire financial problems, so bad that the seminary's creditors were ready to foreclose on the school's property. The day of foreclosure, the president of the seminary and several of his trusted advisors gathered in his office to seek God for miraculous help. As they prayed, one of the faculty named Dr. Harry Ironside lifted up to God, "Lord, we know that the cattle on a thousand hills are yours. Please sell some of them and send us the money."

That prayer may sound strange to your ears, maybe even a bit selfish, but this man was praying honestly from his heart to God. Furthermore, the goal of founding this seminary was to raise generations of educated and trained Christians to spread the gospel of Jesus Christ to the whole world. These people were not praying for their own enrichment; they were praying that the light of Jesus would shine on countless millions of people stuck in the darkness of sin into the far-off future.

What did God do in this situation? Did he answer?

At the same time the prayer meeting was going on, a tall Texan rancher walked into the seminary's business office. Having never been there, he looked around wondering where he should go and who he should speak with, when his eyes fell on the secretary.

Knowing that the deadline for foreclosure was approaching, the secretary nervously looked at the clock on the wall, then sighed heavily before greeting the stranger with an uninterested, "Can I help you?" She wondered what anybody would want from a school that was going under.

The cattleman smiled and removed his hat as he stepped up to her desk. In a strong Texan accent, he said, "Ma'am, this may seem strange, but I just sold two carloads of cattle in Ft. Worth."

Puzzled, the secretary silently stared at the rancher.

He continued, "You see, I've been tryin' to make a business deal, and I was gonna use my money from the sale to make it happen, but it ain't gonna work."

Again, the secretary just listened, wondering what this man wanted.

"You see," he ambled, "I got all this money, but somethin' inside tells me I shouldn't keep it but give it away. I thought and thought about it, and I feel compelled to give it to this school. I don't know if y'all need it or not, but here's the check..."

To the secretary's tremendous shock, the visitor reached into his pocket and pulled out a check, with a lot of zeros on it, written to the school. Overwhelmed with contagious excitement, the secretary jumped up from her chair, thanked the rancher, and ran to the president's office. She paused at the office door when she heard the prayers being offered up inside but then tapped repeatedly on the door for attention.

A bit flustered that someone was interrupting the prayer meeting, the school president cracked open the door and got ready to scold whoever was on the other side. But instead of scolding, his mouth dropped in shock as the secretary pushed the check through the opening and into the president's face.

"God Almighty!" the president exclaimed. "That's exactly how much we owe!"

Now, everyone in the office was interested in what had happened and came over to the door. Examining the check in his hands, the president recognized the cattleman's name. With a chuckle, he turned to Dr. Ironside and said, "Harry, God sold the cattle!"

Ditch Worry

I don't know about you, but worry is one of the easiest things for me to do. My mind can jump to being worried about my wife, my children, my health, my church, my finances, my future, my country, and on and on, in a heartbeat. And this isn't something that just you and I face. Worry is a universal problem for all humans.

The Apostle Paul, who experienced persecution, physical torture, and rejection from his own people, experienced and battled worry. But in Philippians 4:6-7, listen to what he counsels:

> Don't worry about anything; instead, pray about everything; tell God your needs, and don't forget to thank him for his answers. If you do this, you will experience God's peace, which is far more wonderful than the human mind can understand. His peace will keep your

thoughts and your hearts quiet and at rest as you trust in Christ Jesus. (TLB)

Here's a life gamechanger for you: Whenever you start to worry, ditch worry and switch to prayer. I'm serious! Pray with the expectation that God is going to answer, and see what he does!

The level of your *prayerful expectation* will become your level of *peace*.

And don't forget to thank God. Thanking God after he has answered a prayer is gratitude; thanking God BEFORE he answers a prayer is called FAITH. If you have been praying about something for a while and still haven't received an answer, just start thanking God ahead of time for what he is going to do in your life. Many times, we want God to give us something specific, but from his point of view, it would be a much better blessing for him to give us something else. Give him thanks ahead of time; he knows best how to bless.

How about stopping here right now? Think about a problem that you have been praying about. Pause a moment. See it in your mind. Now say this out loud: "Thank you, God, for the answer. I don't know what it is, but you know best; and I thank you for the answer!"

You can take your prayers to a whole new level by praying honestly, continually, and expectantly. Don't forget these three qualities, my friend, because they combine powerfully with the rest of the secrets of prayer that are still to come in the following chapters. Curious about what they are?

Chapter 5

What to Pray

Have you ever been afraid that you might say the "wrong" thing to God when you pray? I have! Maybe you've been hesitant to tell God what you really feel and think about something in fear that it might make him mad at you. Maybe like me, as I was growing in my walk with God, I was scared that if I offended God by saying the wrong thing, he would throw down a bolt of lightning and fry me where I stood!

For a long time, this secret fear worried me because, you see, even though I speak to large crowds regularly, I have a terrible knack for turning an intended compliment into an insult.

Did I Really Say That?!

One Saturday before Easter Sunday, our church was having an Easter egg hunt. My mission during this event was to walk around and meet as many people as possible. Everyone seemed to be having a great time, talking, smiling, laughing, taking pictures, and I was enjoying the moment as well...UNTIL, Rhonda and I walked up to a young couple that I didn't know. They had a young daughter, who was happily swinging an Easter basket. I introduced Rhonda and myself; everything's going great, and THEN I turned to the mother and cheerfully asked, "When's the baby due," with my finger pointed at her stomach.

OMG. Why did I say that?!

Even as the words still lingered in the air, I knew I had made a terrible mistake. Astonished that I'd said that, Rhonda's mouth dropped, while the couple glared back at me with angry faces. The mother snorted, "I've already had my baby! And she's 3 months old!"

I thought, "Congratulations, Jeff, your mouth just destroyed any chance of connecting with this couple." And true to my thought, this family never came back.

So as I'm sure you've observed in your life as well, our words can really make or break relationships. Words are powerful. All throughout the book of Proverbs, words spoken in a gentle, kind, and thoughtful way can bring healing, prosperity, and life, but words spoken in anger, haste, and harshness can, as a great theologian once said, *mess things up!*

So how would God like us to speak to him?

Does it even matter how we talk to him?

I believe that Jesus is the ultimate example to us for how we should pray and talk to God. Jesus demonstrated great respect to God the Father whenever he prayed. His disciples witnessed this unswerving devotion to his Father day after day. And it wasn't always the same prayer.

The disciples heard Jesus pray over 5 loaves of bread and 2 fish. They heard him pray over the sick for healing. They heard him give thanks before meals and heard him give thanks in advance for miracle after miracle. They heard him as he blessed little children, and some of them even heard him pray in the Garden of Gethsemane to the Father, "Let your will be done," as he struggled with the sorrowful anguish of having to go to the cross.

Before one of Jesus' most famous miracles, he arrived at Mary and Martha's house just to learn that their brother Lazarus had died. Jesus was so emotionally moved that he wept and asked to be taken to the tomb of his friend. The event continues as follows in John 11:38-44:

> It was a cave with a stone laid across the entrance. "Take away the stone," he said. "But, Lord," said Martha, the sister of the dead man, "by this time there is a bad odor, for he has been there four days." Then Jesus said, "Did I not tell you that if you believed, you would see the glory of God?" So they took away the stone. Then Jesus looked up and said, "Father, I thank you that you have heard me. I knew that you always hear me, but I said this for the benefit of the people standing here, that they may believe that you sent me." When he said this, Jesus called in a loud voice, "Lazarus, come out!" The dead man came out, his hands and feet wrapped with strips of linen, and a cloth around his face. Jesus said to them, "Take off the grave clothes and let him go."

I find it interesting that Jesus said to the Father, "I knew that you always hear me." To me, this means that even before he arrived at the tomb site, he had already been praying silently within his heart! Imagine: The prayer resulting in the astounding miracle of raising a person from the dead could've been done with only God hearing it.

Now, the disciples were extremely curious about the power of prayer and asked Jesus how to pray so that their prayers would be answered. I'm sure they wondered, "Could God answer our prayers like this as well?"

Back in the Conference Room

To pick up the story where I left off in Chapter 2, I was sitting in a conference room, surrounded by other pastors, and we were captivated by what Dr. Towns' secret to prayer was. After what seemed like a pause that lasted forever, Dr. Towns raised a hand, pointing a finger to heaven as he proclaimed, "God always hears prayers prayed like this: 'Our Father, which art in heaven, hallowed be thy name. Thy kingdom come. Thy will be done in earth, as it is in heaven. Give us this day our daily bread. And forgive us our debts, as we forgive our debtors. And lead us not into temptation, but deliver us from evil: For thine is the kingdom, and the power, and the glory, forever. Amen.'"

If you're like most Americans, you've heard or prayed this prayer somewhere, sometime in your life. Christians of every type refer to it as the "Our Father" or "The Lord's Prayer." You may even be able to recite it! I quoted it here in the King James Version from the book of Matthew, since that's what Dr. Towns used and most of you are familiar with. But there are many English translations of it, all following the intentional pattern of prayer that Jesus gave us.

And, my friend, it's *this pattern* that is the powerful secret of prayer.

Throughout the years, many people have gotten hung up on the *English* translation of this prayer—almost as if the words themselves were like some kind of magic spell that would give the person praying them whatever they wanted. Adding to this, throughout the centuries, other people have fought over whether to say the version of the Lord's

Prayer recorded in the book of Matthew or the one in Luke, which differ slightly in wording.

Let me be clear about this. To begin with, Jesus did not speak English during his ministry with the disciples. Two thousand years ago, *English* did not even exist as a language! Jesus spoke Hebrew, Aramaic, and probably some Greek, and the 4 Gospels were written in Greek, the common language of the time. So to me, fighting over a few English words in a translation of this prayer is silly and completely misses the lesson that Jesus is teaching us through this prayer.

I don't believe that the words in the Lord's Prayer should be the emphasis of our focus in prayer. I believe that the *pattern* of the Lord's Prayer is the secret to powerful, life-changing prayer! I believe that it's a model, a guide for how we should pray. And it's easy enough for a child to learn and use.

Ready to dive deeper into this journey of learning to pray the perfect prayer?

Chapter 6

Recognizing Who God Is

"Our Father"

What comes to your mind when you hear "Our Father?" What emotions are churned up by those two words? Take a moment to think about that before going on.

Since Jesus presents to us through his prayer that God is actually like a father to us, most people then look at God through the lens of how their father treated them growing up and still treat them today. If your earthly father encouraged you as you grew up, showed you mercy when you failed, and cherished you as his child, then chances are extremely high that you'll interact with God like a loving father.

However, if your earthly father harshly punished you for even the smallest mistakes, degraded you in front of others, abandoned you and your family, or withheld his love from you, then chances are high that you are already having a problem envisioning God as a loving father. You may picture God the Father as a divine tyrant, waiting for you to make the slightest mistake so that he can punish you and make your life miserable. My friend, your earthly father may have been (or may still be) an abusive, anger-filled, tormented soul, but your *heavenly* Father is the ultimate, living example of love and mercy.

As my children were growing up, I told them, "God is not like me. I have flaws; he doesn't." And, even though I showed love to my children over and over throughout their childhood and still today, I confess to you that I am not a perfect father. I can get angry very quickly. I can have a stinkin' attitude. I can misunderstand people. And—I don't understand how I do this—I can ruin a very special moment. *Ugh.*

Our heavenly Father, on the other hand, is constant in his love for us—*for you!* Through the Lord's prayer, Jesus was taking his disciples and us by the hand and introducing us to God the Father. "Our" Father, not just Jesus' Father. *Your* heavenly Father, too.

My friend, if we can get past whatever negative examples of fatherhood our earthly fathers set for us, if we can throw out the broken lens that we are trying to see God through and pick up the new one Jesus left for us, we can experience an extraordinary, *real*, day-by-day, loving relationship with God!

And out of this relationship with God, I immediately see three enormous benefits that you can enjoy in your life.

Benefit 1: Freely receiving God's love

You may say, "Jeff, that's easy for you to say, but you don't know what I've been through." You're right; I don't know what you've been through in your life. What I do know is that this is a challenge for ME.

I have struggled to understand how to give and receive love for my whole life. As a child of divorced parents, I felt like my heart was torn apart with every fight, every time I had to pack my suitcase to go live with my other parent, and every time I had to repack my suitcase to go back to the other parent's place. There were so many times I felt like nobody wanted me, like nobody loved me.

By the time I was a preteen, I had 4 younger siblings, and so I was nominated to take care of them while my mom and stepfather worked. Part of me wished that I could receive more attention, as if I were one of the younger children, but I also enjoyed leading my pack of brothers and sisters, and I even occasionally got a "good job" for my efforts!

But when I moved back in with my father, the home dynamic was different. I knew that my dad loved me, but he was so busy with working a full-time job during the day and a side job of repairing and reselling small engines into the night to provide for our family that I felt starved for his attention.

So I started hanging out with him in the evening while he worked on engines, and in my mind, unfortunately, I concluded that love was something to be bartered. If I worked with my father, I felt loved. In my mind, "love" became a commodity that could be bought, sold, or traded.

As I grew into an adult, my belief of love as a "transaction" began to haunt all of my relationships. Just under the surface of all my interactions with people, I believed that if I did something for a person, they should do something equivalent for me—and I kept score in my mind! (You may even think this way.)

I wish I could tell you that when I became a pastor this type of thinking evaporated from my mind and that I was able to love unconditionally as God the Father does, but that didn't happen. Instead, my internal, core belief that love was a transaction threatened my friendships, family life, and almost destroyed my marriage! It wasn't until I was 43 that I finally—*finally*—experienced a breakthrough in my thinking!

Where's My Breakthrough?

One of my friends invited me to a spiritual retreat called *Tres Dias*. I had been previously invited by several people in my church, but I was hesitant to accept the invitation. My friend said, "Jeff, it's just going to be a group of guys who want to grow in serving God. I promise it will change your life." Something about the way he said this flipped a switch in my head, and I found myself agreeing to attend.

As the date of the retreat approached, I felt somewhat apprehensive because I still didn't really know what to expect. When I'd ask people who'd already attended what happens during the retreat, they'd all just get this look in their eyes, smile, and say something like, "I don't want to spoil the surprise. You'll love it!" These words did not soothe my restlessness about this mysterious 3-day getaway at all.

Finally, I arrived at the location, and let me tell you, I gradually experienced a transformative breakthrough in my mind, heart, and spirit. I won't reveal to you exactly what happens at Tres Dias, but I will say that my fears were a complete waste of mental energy. During the 3-day spiritual retreat, the working volunteers, who were not pastors or priests, demonstrated love in a way that I had not encountered before. I'm not talking about mushy stuff; I'm talking about showing love by serving each other just like Jesus showed love toward his disciples. If I tried to help a volunteer with something, they would kindly rebuff me with, "No, just receive."

At first, I struggled to understand the lesson that was being demonstrated for me. "Just receive. Just receive." *Receive what?!* I was perplexed.

When the next day arrived, as our group of random men from all kinds of backgrounds and careers, doctors to farmers, rich to poor, and everyone in between, I started to see men—big men, burly men, men who looked like they could twist steel with their hands—start to openly cry. I remember thinking to myself, *"What is going on over there?"* and *"That's not going to happen to me!"*

Well let me tell you what was going on in those men's minds: They were having a major breakthrough in their lives. After countless years of suffering with private pain and struggles, it was like a rushing river of freedom came sweeping through them, washing away whatever walls were keeping them back from being the person they needed to be.

Ironically, I sat there watching person after person experience an earth-shattering breakthrough—the very thing that I wanted in my life! But I wasn't feeling anything. In fact, I felt quite numb. I started wondering to God, "Where's my breakthrough? I don't feel a thing, God!"

When the retreat ended, I said my goodbyes to the friends I had made and journeyed home. My sponsor's question rattled around in my head: "What did you gain from this weekend?" As the miles swept by, the only reply I could come up with was, "Not a lot of sleep!" We had some snorers in our dorm room, and I had gotten very little sleep on the retreat. I was looking forward to sleeping in my own bed!

That night, as I collapsed into my bed, that question popped back up in my mind: "What did you gain from this weekend?" I finally sighed, "Nothing," rolled over and went to sleep.

The next morning, I rose at my usual time and walked half-asleep to my office for my morning devotion and prayer time. Kneeling down like I had done countless times before, I began praying...but I immediately noticed something! I *felt* God's love for me. I paused in my prayer, shocked by what I was feeling.

I had preached God's love to a multitude of people. I had wept numerous times at Jesus' agony and suffering on the cross. I had read about the love of God in Scripture for years. But suddenly, there, kneeling on the cold wooden floor of my home office, I actually *felt* the warm, glowing, heart-felt love God has for me! Despite my flaws, failures, shortcomings, and mistakes, I felt God's FREELY-GIVEN love! I didn't have to buy, sell, or trade to obtain his love! Hallelujah, this was my BREAKTHROUGH!

In Matthew 10:8, Jesus says, "Freely you have received, freely give." I realized that I couldn't freely give love to others if I couldn't freely receive God's love for me.

My friend, it is my prayer that you learn to accept God's love for you freely. You don't even have to go to a retreat to experience God's love. How you view yourself is not how God views you. He views you by the words of John 3:16: "For God so loved the world that he gave his one and only Son, that whoever believes in him shall not perish but have eternal life."

God's love doesn't waver like ours. His love for us is constant. And I challenge you to receive God's love, even where you are right now!

If you're currently not following Jesus, he would love to shepherd you—guide you through the craziness of this life—and give you the gift of eternal life, a priceless gift made just for you! If you'd like to follow Jesus, here's a simple prayer you can pray to start your walk with him:

> Dear Jesus, I know I'm a sinner. I ask for your forgiveness.
> I believe that you died for my sins and rose from the dead.
> Come into my heart; I want to live for you. Help me to
> turn from my sins and live for you each day. In your holy
> name, I pray. Amen!

If you prayed that prayer, I want to welcome you to God's family! And for everyone reading, let's take a moment to say out loud, "Thank you, God, for loving me!"

Benefit 2: Immediate access to God's throne room

As a follower of Jesus, you can pray anywhere, silently or out loud, "Our Father, who is in heaven." It blows my mind to think that we can enter the throne room of the all-powerful God of the universe through prayer! Think about it: We, little, fragile, mortal humans, CAN walk boldly into heaven's throne room and bow humbly before God's presence through prayer.

God is so beyond-our-imaginations powerful that the Bible says that mountains melt at the mere touch of his presence. Where I live in Georgia, we can see the large granite shape of Stone Mountain for miles. I've visited this mountain park many times throughout my life and climbed the mountain to the top. Standing at the base of the mountain and looking up, its towering presence seems to go on forever. But to think of this mountain melting like a wax candle before God's presence sends chills down my spine thinking about the magnitude of God's power!

And yet, this is the very God who whispers to us in a quiet, small voice: "I love you. Come spend time with me in prayer." I don't know about you, but I want to be on his side and have him fighting for me!

Think about here on this planet, as Americans, we elect a President, and he lives in the White House. The White House is historically known as "the people's house", since our Founding Fathers stressed that we were not ruled by a king but by an elected individual for a limited period of time. But I wouldn't recommend that you just show up and try to walk in without an official appointment. For one thing, you won't even get past the front gate! A host of guards will stop you in your tracks!

Now imagine that you have been granted a special, elite pass that gives you the right to walk right through the gates, across the lawn, in through the doors, down the hallways until you reach the holy of holies in

American culture: The Oval Office. But instead of having to knock on the office door, you just open it, walk in, sit down on a couch, and start talking to the President like old friends. This would be a rare and astounding gift to anybody in the world!

As a Christ follower, you've been given an even GREATER gift than that. You've been granted a universal pass that allows you to walk into God's throne room through prayer 24 hours a day, 7 days a week, for the rest of your life! And you can openly talk to him about anything. ANYTHING!

Disaster!

In 2010, a mining disaster at a gold and copper mine in San Jose, Chili, threatened the lives of 33 miners. A massive boulder in the mine shifted and created an avalanche of stone that blocked all of the tunnels out. The miners were trapped over 2,300 feet underground, almost half a mile! The world watched helplessly on TV and online as pleas for help came from the families of the miners, but the situation looked hopeless.

An American Christian named Greg Hall, who owned a drilling company, was watching the drama play out on TV when he felt an overwhelming desire to help. He journeyed to the site of the mine collapse, organized the massive equipment needed and the operators to work the heavy machinery. But even with a towering drill and a first-class diamond drill bit, boring through 2,300 feet of dense rock was painfully slow.

Days turned into weeks.

Suddenly one day, a horrific screeching erupted from the drill, followed by a low metallic moaning. As white smoke plumed up from the deep hole, Greg knew exactly what had happened, and it was as close to a worst-case scenario as possible. The expensive drill bit had seized in the bedrock!

Exhausted and exasperated by this impossible setback, Greg told God, "Lord, we've done everything we can do. Those are 33 of your children down there. We've done everything we can do. If you want us to get them out, you're going to have to send your holy angels down and dig my bit out, because we're finished!"

Greg signaled to the drill operator to restart the machinery, and miraculously, the frozen drill bit started to move again!

Greg wasn't the only one praying through the crisis. Deep underground, every day after lunch, the miners would gather for prayer. Even though they were separated from the surface by half a mile of solid rock, they knew that God was there with them.

For 69 days, God gave the miners the strength and hope to live in hellish conditions. But he didn't leave them there! He answered their prayers. On the 69th day, video feeds all across the world showed the miners being helped out of the very hole that could've been their grave!

When Greg Hall was interviewed about how he had rescued the miners, he shook his head and replied, "I told everybody that that job couldn't be done. I didn't do that job. God drilled that hole, and I just had a good seat!"

It's estimated that over a billion people, in every part of the world, witnessed the plight of these miners and rejoiced in their rescue. I'd like to add that over a billion people witnessed the power of prayer!

My friend, when you feel like you can't hold it together and it seems like everything is falling apart, the best thing you can do is to trust God and to stay connected to him through prayer.

Prayer is an extraordinary gift we've been given! I encourage you to do it daily!

Benefit 3: A meaningful relationship with the Father

When Jesus taught his disciples how to pray, he could've chosen the words *Lord* or *Master* for them to address the Father—both of which are fine since God *is* our Lord and Master. And in the culture of the time, anyone who served a deity, whether it was the God of Israel or countless other Egyptian, Canaanite, Greek, or Roman gods, understood that we as humans bow before that which we worship. In fact, if you were walking around Israel in Jesus' day, there would've been shrines and temples dedicated to many gods all along the roads of the Roman cities.

The key factor that described all these gods is that they were *impersonal*. You couldn't know them. You couldn't have a relationship with them. In the people's minds, if they didn't somehow please the gods, the gods would randomly kill them by zapping them with a lightning bolt or drowning them at sea or giving them a plague.

Even the Jews, who the one true God had entrusted with his holy Scriptures through Moses and the prophets, mostly had a very cold relationship with God. To them, God's presence was in heaven and also lived in a small room called the Holy of Holies in the Temple in Jerusalem, and only the high priest could go inside this sacred room once a year to ask the Lord to forgive Israel for its sins.

The Bible records a few Jews who developed a close relationship with God through prayer, like Noah, Abraham, Moses, David, and Daniel. But in general, most of the Israelites believed that God was too powerful and great for them to ever get really close to. They believed it was their duty to *fear* God.

But Jesus Says...

With all of that in mind, Jesus shatters millennia of human misconceptions about God by saying that we should begin our prayers with *"Our Father."* I can't stress to you strongly enough how RADICAL this idea was and still is! Our. Father.

And that's just the English wording. In Aramaic, which was the common people's language in Israel during Jesus' time, Jesus said *"Abba."* Jewish children used Abba as a term of endearment for their father and is best translated into English as "Papa" or "Daddy." You can imagine that in Jesus' day, when a father returned home from working, his children would run out to him, saying "Abba!" over and over.

Jesus immediately puts a picture in our minds that God wants us to have a close, compassionate, father-child relationship with him. And as spiritual children, we don't need special permission to talk to our Father. We can do this any time. We can run to him in prayer, saying, "Papa, let me tell you about today..."

We shouldn't fear him. In Romans 8:15 (CEV), Paul declares that, "God's Spirit doesn't make us slaves who are afraid of him. Instead, we become his children and call him our Father."

The Boy Vs. the Guard

I read a story about an emperor whose army had won a great victory against an enemy. The emperor orchestrated a parade to celebrate his triumph over his foe. As the emperor led the grand procession through the streets of his grand city, a little boy plowed his way through the crowd that lined the way. Just as the boy was about to run up to the emperor's chariot, a guard caught sight of the potential danger to the emperor and snatched the child back out of the street.

Agitated, the guard scolded, "Boy, do you know who that is in that chariot?!" Before the child could answer, the guard emphasized, "He is the *emperor*!"

The boy rubbed his nose and then returned the guard's stern look with such strength of conviction that it startled the guard. Pointing to the chariot, the boy replied, "He might be your emperor, but he's *my* father!"

Our Heavenly Father

God is our heavenly Father. God is *your* heavenly Father. I don't know how close your relationship is with him, but I encourage you to grow that relationship. Just like you'd feed plants with water and nutrients to grow them, feed your relationship with God with time for prayer each day. Even if it's just for 5 minutes or an hour or times scattered throughout the day, the most important thing is to invest in your relationship with him daily.

He wants to spend time with you! I promise you that he's waiting for you to talk to him, despite anything that you've done. He has mercy and forgiveness waiting for you. Go to him. Spend time with our Father. It'll change your life!

Always let the phrase "Our heavenly Father" remind you that God loves you no matter what.

Chapter 7

The Prayer of Respect

"Hallowed be your name"

Growing up, whenever I'd hear the word *hallowed* in church, I thought the pastor was saying *hollowed*, as in hollowing out a hole in a piece of wood. You can imagine the confusing and comical picture in my mind as I visualized God with a giant hole in his torso. The only other word in my young vocabulary that sounded similar was *Halloween*, and that definitely didn't make any sense to me!

As an adult, I don't think I've ever heard anyone use the word *hallowed* in conversation, except when reciting the Lord's Prayer. So let me fill you in on the meaning of this now rare word. To hallow something is to show the utmost respect and honor for it. It's to consecrate something as the epitome of holiness and all that is sacred.

Here in America, we tend to look back on great people from our history, like Abraham Lincoln and Martin Luther King, Jr., with an air of awe and reverence. We hallow their names as leaders who helped reshape American culture and society. Around the world, Mother Teresa is remembered for her extraordinary compassion for the sick and dying, caring for the outcasts who nobody cared for and nobody wanted. She has been hallowed by countless as a shining example of God's mercy and love, and the Catholic Church further hallowed her name by canonizing her as a saint after her death.

Hopefully these modern examples help you start to feel the type of reverence Jesus said that we should give to God when we pray. Now, I want to take you back to Jesus' time for an ancient example of just how much the Jews respected the name of God.

The Name of God

Have you ever heard, "You shall not take the name of the Lord your God in vain?" I guarantee that 99% of you have heard this verse in some form during your life. It's the 3rd Commandment, and from ancient times to today, the Jews have taken this commandment very seriously.

The Hebrew word that our English versions translate as *Lord* or *God* was so hallowed by Jews that most would not say the word out loud but would instead substitute a different word for fear that they would accidentally misuse the name of God and thereby break the 3rd Commandment.

And get this! Jewish scribes had extensive rules that they had to follow (and still do) whenever they were making copies of the Hebrew Bible. They hallowed the Scriptures as the Word of God and did everything humanly possible to reverence the text as a living document.

When a scribe copying the Bible came to the name of God in the text, he would stop and put down his quill. Depending upon the rules of the scribes, he may have to get up, walk to the nearest pool for ceremonial cleansing, and then return to the scriptorium to present himself to the Lord as a clean vessel. Only then would he be viewed as worthy enough to write God's name.

When other scribes came to God's name in the scroll they were copying, they'd put down their quill, pick up a different one, carefully write the name of the Lord, and then break the quill so that it couldn't be used for any other purpose! When you consider how limited writing supplies were back then, that's a pretty big sacrifice just to write one word. But the Jews hallowed that one word more than all other words in existence.

If the scribe made a mistake in copying a page, he had to correct it immediately or his hours of back-bending work were in jeopardy of being ruined! If, when checked by the editor, the scroll contained more than 3 errors or even just 1 error that couldn't be corrected, the entire scroll—months of meticulous work—could be buried, never to be used by anyone!

I hope this gives you a taste of how the Jews of Jesus' day reverenced God.

Now, I know that you're not handwriting copies of the Bible in Hebrew. But I tell you that you have the freedom as a follower of Christ to do something that ancient scribes could only dream of doing: You can give reverence to God directly to him in your times of prayer.

You may say, "That's great, Jeff. I want to hallow God's name and show him respect and honor...but, *how* do I do that exactly?"

Let me help you with this. Here are 3 ways that will help you to show respect to God while praying or in your mind any time of the day. There are literally an infinite number of ways that we can worship and extend our reverence to God, but let these 3 be a starting place for you to then branch out from as you grow in your relationship with God!

Way of Respect 1: Believe that God exists

You may not have noticed this, but as you read the Bible, it never attempts to prove that God exists. Some of you just stopped reading and thought, "What?!?" Yes! It's true. The Bible doesn't try to give you a debate argument, with 23 points, 72 parables, diagrams, and a PowerPoint presentation, to prove that God exists. From the beginning, the Bible proclaims that God IS. No debate, no TED Talk, no council of scholars wrangling for centuries over whether God exists or not. No.

It's Obvious

From the Bible's perspective, the existence of God is self-evidently obvious just from the complexity of the world around us and from the miracle of life itself! The Bible is set in a context that God not only exists but HAS TO exist for the universe to have been made and to be sustained!

It's like the well-told story of a man walking across a field one day after the torrential rains of a storm had flooded the area with debris. Eyeing the ground as he walked, he caught sight of something partially buried under a clump of mud. Stooping down, he brushed aside the mud and smiled as he saw the glint of metal and glass from a pocket watch. Extracting the watch from the muck, he dangled it in front of him by its chain and had a flash of obvious but genius insight: If there was a watch, there had to be a watchmaker.

Scientists have calculated that our planet is approximately 93 million miles away from the sun and rotates at a tilt of 23.5 degrees, both of which bless our planet with just the right amount of heat and light so that life can flourish all over the globe. We take it for granted when we go outside that life is all around us: trees, vegetation, animals, insects, people. But if our planet was nearer to the sun, life would be jeopardized by extreme heat. If the earth were further away from the sun, we'd be in danger of colder temperatures and less light, neither good for plants. And if plants can't survive on this planet, we're goners!

I don't believe for a second that the earth is where it is by accident, and the Bible doesn't either. The Bible's classic opening line in Genesis 1:1 declares, "In the beginning, God created the heavens and the earth." I fully believe that if there is a watch, like in the earlier story, there has to be a watchmaker. I believe that God created our world and the universe.

Hebrews 11:6 states, "And without faith it is impossible to please God, because anyone who comes to him must believe that he exists and that he rewards those who earnestly seek him." God rewards us when we give respect to him.

During my prayer time, I find ways to express my reverence and honor for him with expressions like "I praise you, God, for who you are" and "I glorify you for what you have done in my life and what you can do." I don't hallow God's name with these same words every time I pray. I find different ways to show my love and gratitude toward God. So when you pray, I encourage you to be creative here. Don't just say the same things over and over. Speak from your heart to God about how much you honor him, and the Bible promises that he will honor you!

Way of Respect 2: Remember that his name represents his power

You may have heard a preacher say, "God doesn't have a last name!" You've *definitely* heard what people around you think his last name is!

I love to play golf. And a lot of times, I'll play with people who are not Christ followers. If you're not a fan of golf, you may think, "What's the big deal about hitting a little ball across a field into a hole?" I actually thought that at one point in my life...until I started playing it!

Golf is actually quite difficult. A golfer has to judge the distance to a tiny hole in the ground far, far away. Wind direction, which club to use, how much force to put into the swing—all of these are going through a golfer's mind while everyone else is standing around watching. And every golf course is different. Even the pros can make huge mistakes during any given game.

So when one of the people I'm playing with tees off and the ball goes whistling through the air and then, *PLUNK*, lands in the water or a sand trap or the woods, I usually get to hear them call out to God...but they get his last name wrong.

I'm all about loving and reaching out to people, but I can't stand hearing people misuse God's name. It makes me cringe. So I'll speak up, not in a harsh way, but request that they don't curse God while we're together. And you know what, most of the times I speak up, the person stops cursing and apologizes for talking about my Father that way in front of me.

The Most Expensive Bird in the World

I heard a story one time of a man who grew up in a poor family but who had a dream of becoming a business owner. When he started his business, it didn't go well at first, but as he continued to apply his hard work to the endeavor, his business began to flourish.

With cash multiplying in his bank account, he decided he wanted to do something nice for his mother. He thought, "Mom's rather lonely, so I'll buy her a bird to keep her company." He looked and looked for just the right bird to get his mother, and finally made an extraordinary discovery! He found a bird that could dance, sing, and even talk!

He cheerfully paid the exorbitant price of $5,000 for the bird; after all, he wanted to bless his mother with a unique gift. And then he thought, "I know! I'll surprise her by shipping the bird to her! I wish I could see her face when her doorbell rings, she answers it, and there on her front porch is this one-of-a-kind bird, singing, dancing, and talking to her!"

He contacted a shipping service, and the courier collected the bird along with a hastily scribbled note that read, "Mom, I hope you enjoy this gift."

And then, the son didn't hear anything.

For days, he kept expecting his phone to ring with his mother on the other end. After five days of anxious waiting, he finally called his mother. When she answered, he blurted out, "Mom! Did you get the gift I sent you?"

There was a pause on the other line, followed by a cheerful, "Oh, yes! Yes, I did receive your gift, son! Thank you so much! I enjoyed it immensely! That was the tastiest bird I've ever cooked!"

His mouth dropping open in horror, the son stammered, "B-b-but... that bird cost $5,000! It could sing and dance and talk!"

On the other end, his mother chuckled and replied, "Well if that was the case, that bird should've spoken up!"

The Great I AM

In the Old Testament, we read that after Moses fled Egypt's royal house as a young man and then tended flocks in the desert wilderness for decades, God appeared to Moses through a burning bush and called him to a special mission: to free the Jews from captivity in Egypt. But Moses was troubled. He had already fled Egypt for his life, and he didn't think that even the Jews he was trying to rescue would accept him. He begged God for a way to prove to the Jews that he was truly sent by the one true God. So he asked God what name he should use. And God gave a fascinating response, recorded in Exodus 3:14:

God replied to Moses, "I AM WHO I AM." Say this to the people of Israel: I AM has sent me to you."

One of the powerful things God was saying to the Jews is, "I am whatever you will need me to be." And the book of Exodus demonstrates God's commitment to protect and provide for the children of Israel over and over. As they traveled through the barren wilderness, God miraculously provided food in the form of *manna* and quail for them, water from rock, a cloud to cool them during the heat of the day, a pillar of fire to warm them at night, and even extended the life of their clothing and sandals.

The I AM was more than enough for the Jews as they left Egypt, and I can tell you from personal experience that God is STILL more than enough for his followers. Jesus even references God's blessings during the journey out of Egypt when speaking about his divine nature in John 6:48-51:

> "I am the bread of life. Your forefathers ate the manna in
> the desert, yet they died. But here is the bread that comes
> down from heaven, which a man may eat and not die.
> I am the living bread that came down from heaven. If
> anyone eats of this bread, he will live forever. This bread
> is my flesh, which I will give for the life of the world."

Jesus goes even further by claiming that he is the I AM of ancient Israel in John 14:6 when he says, "I AM the way the truth and the life. No one comes to the Father except through me." Jesus carries on his Father's name, and when we pray "Hallowed be your name," it reminds us of God's unbounded, miraculous power to be the help we need, when we need it. He is the great I AM.

Way of Respect 3: Give praise to God

Jesus gave us a beautifully simple yet intentional guide to prayer, and it flows from one thought into the next. He began with saying "Our Father," reminding us of God's love, then followed with "Hallowed be your name." In this order, before we even start asking God for help or forgiveness, we start by acknowledging that he *has* the power to help and forgive us. From the very beginning, we declare to the world that God is capable of doing anything and that his heart for us is boundless. And that sets up in our minds that God *can* and *will* help his followers.

Most of us begin our prayers asking God to forgive our sins. If you know the Lord's prayer, you know that asking for forgiveness shows up much later in the prayer. I believe it's because God wants us to focus on his love for us and how good he is *before* we focus on how bad we've been.

Remember that God is always good even when we feel like he should be mad at us. There are consequences for our wrongdoings, but they don't change how much God loves you. He is for us even when we seem to be against him.

And the Walls Came Down

In the book of Joshua, Joshua was the leader and general of the Israelites who survived the wilderness journey out of Egypt. God had told them that he was giving them the land of Canaan, but that they would have to fight for it. God even miraculously parted the waters of the flooded Jordan River for the Israelites. But when they saw the walls of the city Jericho, they froze with fear!

The walls of this city towered over the plain. Its walls were so thick, that houses and apartments were built on top of them! Furthermore, word of the approaching mass of Israelites had already reached Jericho's leaders, and they had shut and secured the city's massive doors. The Israelites had no siege engines, catapults, or battering rams. They had no super-tall ladders that would help their fighters scale the walls. To their eyes, this city was impenetrable!

Joshua was a man who believed in prayer, and that's exactly what he turned to when faced with this seemingly impossible obstacle. But Joshua 6:2 records that God spoke to Joshua and gave him the exact battle plan to use to take the city. The only problem with God's plan was that it didn't really seem like much of a battle plan.

God told Joshua to have the people silently march around the city once a day, for 6 days. He also told Joshua to put the priests carrying the Ark of the Covenant in the front of the line. The priests were also to blow trumpets of ram's horns as they walked. But on the 7th day, God instructed that the people would march 7 times around the city, and at the end of the 7th time around, the people were to shout loud praises to God.

To any ancient or modern tactician, this battle plan looks dangerously silly at best. Nevertheless, Joshua knew that he had heard from God, and he instructed the people of Israel to do exactly as God has communicated. And they did!

For 7 days, the Israelites marched around the city, and on the 7th, they marched 7 times, and at the end of the 7th time around, Joshua 6:20 describes what happened next:

> When the trumpets sounded, the people shouted, and at the sound of the trumpet, when the people gave a loud shout, the wall collapsed; so every man charged straight in, and they took the city.

It was the shout of praise to God that brought Jericho's walls down and brought a great victory for the Israelites, and I say to you that *praise* still brings walls down! Instead of walls of stone, I'm talking about walls of disappointment and depression, walls of rejection and uncertainty, walls of fear and hopelessness. Praising God fills us with the courage to conquer the Jericho's in our lives!

When praise goes up, discouragement comes down!

Praise Up an Answer

Back during the recession of 2009, my friend Pastor Evadne Knight started meeting with people in her home to pray on a weekly basis. That prayer meeting grew into a church gathering on Sundays. After having church in her home for several months, the young congregation began to hunt for a building of their own to have service in.

They found a building for sale for an excellent price, but it needed to be extensively remodeled, which wasn't a problem for the young church. They had connections to contractors who were very eager to help them transform the property into a church...IF, they could get the county to issue the proper permits.

Days turned into weeks and then months, as the county code enforcement officer delayed issuing the permits. Every time it seemed like the church was going to get a green light to start renovations, they'd suddenly get a red light from county code enforcement.

Finally, it came down to an important meeting with the code enforcement officer, the building inspector, the fire marshal, and Pastor Knight. It looked like the whole building program was going to be delayed again, but Pastor Knight had a secret ally, a person who outranked everybody involved in the meeting. That morning, she arrived at the building before anyone else and started calling out to God in prayer.

As people started arriving, she continued walking around the building proclaiming praises like, "God, I praise you because this building is yours. God, I praise you because hurting people will give their lives to you and you will heal them. God, I praise you because this building belongs to you! This is not my building or the county's building; it's yours!"

Despite the vacant and shocked looks from the code officer, building inspector, and fire marshal, she continued on in a loud voice, now thanking God for their service to the community and praying a hedge of protection over them and their families.

As Pastor Knight walked to another part of the building, continuing to praise God and pray for the county, the code officer, building inspector, and fire marshal exchanged glances and began mediating among themselves what needed to be done. When Pastor Knight returned to the lobby, the code officer greeted her with a smile and a shake of his head. He said, "Pastor, I don't think anyone has ever prayed for my family like that. I'll make sure you get your permit by the end of the week."

To this I say, "Hallelujah!"

When opposition says there is no way, God can change hearts and even turn the opposition into an ally! Praising God can transform your darkness into light, sorrow into joy, and hopelessness into excited anticipation! Hallowed be your name, Father!

My friend, I believe that he can do for you far more than you can imagine if you will just take the time to pray and praise him!

Hallowed be your name.

Chapter 8

The Prayer of Surrender

"Your Kingdom come, your will be done
on earth as it is in Heaven"

When Jesus was asked what is the greatest commandment, his response in Luke 10:27 was, "Love the Lord your God with all your heart and with all your soul and with all your strength and with all your mind, and love your neighbor as yourself." What are the heart, soul, and mind that Jesus refers to here?

John Ortberg in his book *Soul Keeping* explains that our heart is our will, our choices; our mind is our thoughts and desires, and our strength is our body.

These three things working together form who we are as a person. The heart, soul, and mind combine to form the core of what separates us from animals and distinguishes us as human beings, God's special creation. Genesis declares that God made us in his likeness, and I believe that these three things echo the triune nature of our Creator.

Not My Will

Just as our "will" shows the intent and motivation of our heart, our will naturally shows up in the choices we make day to day. Since most of us live our days on autopilot, going about the routines and habits we've set up without much thought, you might be surprised that the decisions you make throughout your day reveal the things that are the most important to you. Collectively, your daily choices proclaim your *will*.

So when Jesus tells us to love the Lord with all our heart, we need to stop for a moment and ask ourselves, "How do I show my love for God?" I believe that we demonstrate our love for God by the choices we make, and NOT just by following *our* will.

Once again, showing us the example of how we should live our lives, Jesus' gut-wrenchingly emotional prayer in the Garden of Gethsemane recorded in Luke 22:42 contradicts modern, life-success "experts" who say that we should do what we want to do, whenever we want. Listen to Jesus' authentic openness and humbleness as he prays to the Father:

"Father, if you are willing, take this cup from me; yet not my will, but yours be done."

This simple, one sentence prayer is one of the most earth-shaking statements in the Bible. It pulls back the curtain on the relationship between Jesus and his heavenly Father. Jesus knows that his betrayal and crucifixion are rapidly approaching that very night, and his humanness is begging that God find another way to make a path to salvation available for all humanity. The Bible says that Jesus was so overwhelmed by such intense emotions during this prayer time in the garden that he sweated blood!

And I don't fault him at all for asking God to find another way if it were possible. I mean, who would want to be made fun of in front of a crowd of soldiers, who beat you and whipped you and rammed thorns into your head and then made you carry a heavy wooden post to then nail your hands and feet to a cross and leave you there in unimaginable agony to slowly die from suffocation or heart failure? Do you blame Jesus for wanting to avoid all that cruelty if it were possible? I sure don't.

But here's the shocker; here's the amazing example that Jesus left for us: Despite his plea for God to take away his approaching suffering, he ended his appeal with, "yet not my will, but yours be done."

Just sit with that thought for a moment to feel the gravity of Jesus' submission to the will of the Father.

Plans to Prosper You

When we pray, "Your will be done on earth as it is in heaven," we are bowing to God, saying, "Have your way God."

We may think we know what's best for us, and we may think we know how God should answer our prayers. But I can tell you with 100% certainty that God knows what's best for us. His unfathomably infinite mind comprehends every potential impact of every possible option that you can choose from every second of every day of your life and the end result of every decision tree available to you and every person on this planet, all instantly in his mind. My friend, I can assure you that God knows what's best for you and the best way to answer your prayers.

And the great news from Jeremiah 29:11 is that this all-powerful and all-knowing God is not coldly distant but loves you *individually* and has *good* plans for your life.

"For I know the plans I have for you," declares the Lord, "plans to prosper you and not to harm you, plans to give you hope and a future."

Wow! God has plans to give you a hopeful future in which you prosper and are not harmed! I can truly say that we are at our best when we say "yes" to God's will!

I challenge you to pray daily, "Have your way with me and my life, God."

How We Can Surrender to God

Just as Jesus surrendered to the will of the Father, we can surrender to God daily in 3 major areas of our life.

1. Let go of the need for control

Every day, when we rise in the morning, we have to decide who's going to be in control of our life: us or God? Most if not all of us struggle in some way with trying to control the people and world around us as well as our own self. It's very easy to turn to negative emotions and tactics like anger, manipulation, bullying, and lying to get what we want from others. At some point, we all come into contact with a person who yells or explodes in a fiery tantrum if anyone disagrees with them. You may have even been this person at times in your life. I confess that I have! Most people have to "walk on eggshells" around people who act this way.

There are also people who take the opposite approach and try to do everything it takes to make others happy. Because they don't want anyone to be upset, they will go to any length imaginable to placate and calm others, hoping that those people will then give them special favors. Yep, I've done this, too, in my life. It ties back to my old difficulty I spoke about in a previous chapter about bartering service and gifts for someone's love and loyalty.

You might say, "What's wrong with being nice to people?" There's nothing wrong with being nice to people; on the contrary, Jesus *wants* us to show love to everyone—people we know and complete strangers. The problem I'm referring to here is the MOTIVE behind the action. If you do something nice for a person to show them God's love, that's awesome! Keep doing it! But, if you're secretly trying to "butter" people up to get your way, you may want to take a serious inward look at *why* you feel you need to act that way. What's your motive? Are you trying to control someone?

Flowing from that thought, here's a big question to ponder: **Am I trying to control God?**

For you, that question may have been like a giant boulder splashing into a quiet pond. But it's a question we must all consider. Why? Because there is room for only one God to be God, and if we're trying to control him, that means that we are ultimately trying to become God. And my friend, you and I are definitely *not* God!

A much better, freer, more relaxed way of life is to stop trying to control other people and God. Let go of them! (In truth, you don't really control them anyway.) Instead, surrender to God daily. Bring your pain, problems, and discouragement to him. You may even need to surrender to God several times throughout the day. As I'm sure you've experienced, things can come at you from all directions at any time of the day or night. So, if you're starting to feel stressed or want to reach out and seize control of someone or some situation, run to God instead. Tell him, "I surrender to you, Father. Your kingdom come; your will be done."

> "Be still and know that I am God; I will be exalted among the nations. I will be exalted in the earth." -Psalm 46:10

2. Choose contentment

Learning to be content is another way that we can surrender to God. But a lot of times in modern America, this can be difficult. Countless companies are constantly pushing an inconceivable variety of food, clothes, jewelry, electronics, vehicles, houses, vacations, fitness equipment, and so on at you, and if you don't have the money at the moment, they're more than happy to lend you the credit to fill up your home with mountains of stuff! Add to this the continuous stream of social media, updating you on what your family and friends and coworkers have recently purchased or the trip to sunny paradise they took while you worked in a dreary office, and let's face it: Contentment can be tough sometimes.

Contentment is an intentional choice we must make. Don't believe me? Listen to what the Apostle Paul said in Philippians 4:11-13 (NCV):

> I have learned to be satisfied with the things I have and with everything that happens. I know how to live when I am poor, and I know how to live when I have plenty. I have learned the secret of being happy at any time in everything that happens, when I have enough to eat and when I go hungry, when I have more than I need and when I do not have enough. I can do all things through Christ, because he gives me strength.

Wow! In case you're not familiar with the life of Paul, this guy was shipwrecked 3 times, beaten by crowds, whipped by the Roman soldiers, robbed, falsely accused, stoned almost to death, threatened with torture, cold, hungry, thirsty, sick, and abandoned by his friends...

...and he wrote the passage above not in some fancy hotel but *from jail!*

And despite all of that suffering, Paul says that he has found the secret of being happy at any time. Through his life, he learned to choose contentment over the trials that dogged his life. He accepted the things that he couldn't change and trusted God to handle them.

Contentment is a choice for us to make.

I'm in Donut Heaven

As we talk about contentment, I must confess that I love Krispy Kreme donuts. I don't get very excited about a lot of things in life, but when I even just think the words *Krispy Kreme*, my mouth starts salivating and my heart beats a little faster. I used to have to travel far to find a location to purchase some of these little drops of glazed heaven, but then they opened up a store near my home! Oh, my, my, my!

Sometimes, while driving by the donut shop with my wife Rhonda in the car, we'll see in big, red neon letters the word "Hot" on the store sign. Rhonda and I will exchange a quick glance, and I'll make a course correction for the store's parking lot!

Once inside, I'll press my face up to the glass wall, like a puppy dog, where I can watch the donuts being made right in front of me. Flour, salt, eggs, and sugar are all carefully mixed together into a batter that is precisely formed into the donut shape and dropped on a conveyor that drops and flips them in a lazy river of hot grease. The little rafts of goodness then rise out of their crispy bath and get a shower from a waterfall of sugary icing. *Ummmm!*

The workers then scoop them up one by one and gently place them in a box for sale, and I cheerfully plunk down some greenbacks on the counter to buy them. Rhonda and I will then take a seat in the dining area and savor every moment as those little bites of heavenly manna melt in my mouth!

You may be thinking right now, "What does all of that have to do with contentment?! Now I want to go buy a dozen donuts!"

I share that story with you for two important reasons. First, if I didn't practice contentment regularly in my diet, I could literally go crazy eating Krispy Kreme donuts. Donuts for breakfast; donuts for lunch; donuts for dinner; donuts for dessert (of course!). But it wouldn't be long before my lack of restraint and contentment would start impacting my health negatively. I don't care how much you exercise; you can't out exercise a diet of just donuts!

The second reason I shared that story is that God is taking all things in your life—even the bad ones—and turning them into something beautiful. Take the donut for instance: flour, salt, eggs, and sugar. Have you ever tasted flour by itself? *Yuck!* Eat too much salt and...well...you'd die. Even the thought of eating raw eggs grosses me out, and too much sugar...well... that could kill you, too, eventually.

But something magical happens during the cooking process that transforms these unappetizing ingredients into a tasty wonder!

My friend, that is what God does with our failures, our pain, our misery, our mistakes, our sorrow. Somehow, God gathers these wounds we suffer in life and melds them into something new, something that changes us, something that helps us help others, something that brings him glory, just like Paul says in Romans 8:28:

> And we know that in all things God works for the good
> of those who love him, who have been called according
> to his purpose.

God is taking all the things in your life and working them into something truly marvelous. If you get hung up on an unfortunate event in your life, you may never find true contentment. You may feel like God has ignored or failed you. My friend, if that is how you feel, I want to encourage you to let go of those things that you cannot control. None of us can control the things in our past; they've already passed. We live on with the memories and consequences, but we can also give these over to God, knowing that we have his promise that he is turning them into something good down the road.

Contentment is a choice, and you can get started on making that decision daily when you pray, "Your will be done."

I can do all things through Christ who strengthens me.
-Philippians 4:13 (NKJV)

3. Trust God with your future

For most of my life, I've struggled with the fear of death. When I was a child, I witnessed my brother's death, and that traumatic moment has haunted me for decades. Many times in my life, I've noticed that as my fear rises, so does my anxiety level.

On one particular day some years ago, I found myself overwhelmed with anxiety. I tried to pray, tried to listen to worship music, tried to read the Bible, but the fight or flight reflex inside of me was out of control. I was on the verge of physically shaking when I asked Rhonda to take me to see a counselor I had visited a couple of times.

As we rode along, I kept praying, "God, you've gotta help me. God, I love you, and I need your help."

Once we arrived at the office and I followed my counselor to his room, I sank into a chair, with a pad and pen ready to take notes. I just knew that my counselor was going to fix me. I believed that he had some kind of special technique or phrase for me to say that was going to ward off my anxiety and help me continue on my mission of reaching my community for Christ.

After I poured out my heart to him, telling him everything about the storm that was raging around me, he sat back in his chair and then leaned forward, locking his eyes with mine. I swallowed nervously. It seemed like his eyes were piercing straight through to my soul!

In a calm but firm voice, he declared, "Jeff, I think I see the root of your problem. You don't trust anyone, not even God."

I was floored!

I defensively shot back, "How can you say I don't trust God? I read the Bible daily, pray daily, and I've been a pastor for 12 years! How dare you tell me I don't trust God!"

That session was over. I stomped out of the office and told myself, "I'll never go back to him again!"

But as I rode home and my adrenaline subsided, I started thinking about what my counselor had said. Watching the trees alongside the road blur by my window, I suddenly found myself nodding. "He's right," I mentally confessed. "He's right. I don't trust people...and I guess I don't really trust you, God."

The words of Jesus from John 14:1 came to mind:

> "Do not let your hearts be troubled. Trust in God; trust
> also in me."

My friend, Jesus gives the cure to anxiety in this verse. To present your heart from being troubled, put your trust in God. Put your trust in Jesus.

I admit to you that there are still times where I find myself starting to spiral down into the pit of anxiety, especially when resistance and opposition far out of my control come at me from all directions. Those types of situations stress out most if not all of us at times. The key to making it through those times is to let go of trying to control everyone and everything and to put your trust in God.

And it's a process of growing into this trust. It's a journey that we choose to take for the rest of our lives. But here's something to encourage you: The more often you choose to put your trust in God, the easier it becomes to do so down the road.

For instance, where I am in my walk with God now, I recognize when those anxiety-triggering thoughts start to rise within me. Instead of feeding those thoughts, I starve them by going to God in prayer and saying, "Your will be done, Father. I trust you." And I can literally feel my anxiety going down.

Trust, like forgiveness, is not a feeling but a minute by minute choice.

God's Got It

I was greeting people after a service one Sunday, and I shook the hand of a young man I had known for some time. I also knew about struggles that he was having, but he greeted me with one of the brightest smiles I've ever seen. It was like he had suddenly tapped a well of confidence and joy.

After shaking hands, he pulled up his sleeve, revealing a tattoo that read, "God's Got It." I stared at it a moment and then chuckled, "Man, I need that tattooed on my forehead!"

Now, I'm *not* recommending that you go out and get a tattoo of "God's Got It." Please do not come up to me after a service with it tattooed on your forehead, because that is NOT what I'm saying here.

What I am saying is to imprint those words in your mind! God's. Got. It. Solomon, who was one of the wisest people to ever live, proclaims in Proverbs 3:5-6:

> Trust in the Lord with all your heart and lean not on your
> own understanding; in all your ways acknowledge him,
> and he will make your paths straight.

Instead of panicking in the face of your problems, confidently declare Hebrews 13:6: "The Lord is my helper; I will not be afraid!"

Palms Up

Here's an exercise you can also do whenever you start to feel overwhelmed with stress. Think of all your stress and problems. Now take your hands with palms up and raise them up about waist high, as if you're holding in your hands all those problems.

Now close your hands like a fist and turn your hand over; then open your hands with palms down as you release your problems to God. End by turning your hand back over with palms up and say, "God, I surrender; your will be done."

My friend, if you apply these truths to your life daily, I promise you that you'll begin to see great changes in your emotions, relationships, and mental outlook!

By praying to "our Father" and "hallowing his name" and learning to release your need for control by praying "your will be done," you are then ready to discover and apply the next key treasure within Jesus' amazing model prayer.

Chapter 9

The Prayer of Provision

"Give us this day our daily bread"

One thing that is universal for all of us is our *inability* to see the future. It doesn't matter where you live, how much education you've had, or how much is in your bank account, none of us know what tomorrow will bring. We may have plans for tomorrow; we may have a daily routine we follow; we may have listened to the weather forecast the night before and think we know exactly what's going to happen.

But as we all know, unexpected events crop up in our lives all the time...unexpectedly. Even with the fanciest supercomputers churning through countless calculations, weather forecasters can still get weather prediction wrong. How many times have you planned an outdoor event, just to have a random cloud rain on it? As a pastor who has performed many outdoor weddings, I can testify that, "yes," weather forecasters are not always right!

We can take guesses about what's going to happen. We can look at the past and try to predict general trends of what will happen, but we never know *exactly* what's right around the corner for us every minute of every day of our lives. So nod if you could use God's favor in your day to day life. (I'm nodding my head!)

We may not see what's coming for our lives, but God does. The future, past, and present are all open and revealed to God. Nothing takes God by surprise; he already knows what will happen. Wouldn't it help you to breathe a little easier each day to know that you had a guide in your life who already knows the path you will walk?

When we pray, "Give us this day our daily bread," we are confessing to God, "I need your help, God, today. Give me what I need for this day."

I'm Hungry!

Today in modern America, food is bountifully produced and available in some form on almost every street corner. Food is so plentiful, that one of the biggest problems facing Americans is overeating and obesity. So when we read "daily bread," our minds kind of gloss over how extremely important bread and simple foods were to our ancestors.

For most of time, humans have woken up every morning with only one thing on their minds: where am I going to get food to feed myself and my family today?

Throughout millennia, if you didn't hunt it, grow it, or barter for it, you'd go hungry and eventually starve to death. And you don't have to go back too far to experience this desperation over food. My grandparents had to endure the Dust Bowl era and depression of the 1930s, when families, like yours and mine, didn't know where the next meal was coming from. To be given a fresh loaf of bread every day would be like a treasure coming down from heaven. This scarcity of food was true during Jesus' day as well.

Suddenly, Jesus' prayer, "Give us this day our *daily bread*," becomes tremendously more powerful! And I don't think Jesus was limiting this part of his prayer to bread and food. I believe that Jesus was encouraging us to trust in God to give us *whatever we need for the day*.

Let's face it: Just because we become a Christ follower does NOT mean that all of our days are going to be problem-free, sunny, walking-on-air days! So, if you're a new follower of Jesus or have been following his teachings for years, don't get disillusioned when troubles come your way. The Bible is clear that struggles, trials, and tribulations will come our way, but the amazing game changer for each of us is that we do not have to go through these challenges alone! God is with us!

Jesus said it this way in John 16:33:

> "I have told you these things, so that in me you may have peace. In this world you will have trouble. But take heart! I have overcome the world."

Jesus says that despite the craziness that we experience in this world that we can still experience inner peace. How? By us putting our confidence in God. Why? To paraphrase Jesus' sentiment here: "Because I've beatin' every single thing that can come against you, and I am the triumphant King of this world! So there! Take that Satan!"

I don't know about you, but it gives me peace just knowing that I'm following the only one in history who has the power to triumph over death itself! If we were picking teams, I'm like, "I want to be on *that* guy's side because I want him fighting for me!"

God, give me what I need today!

To help you deepen your daily prayer life, I'm going to share with you 3 important ways that you can receive this "daily bread."

1. Recognize God as the source of your life.

Life in our universe comes directly from God. Genesis records that in the beginning, God created everything from NOTHING.

You may ask, "How can you make something out of nothing?" My answer is simple: We can't! This is something that only God can do.

Through the marvels of chemistry, scientists can create exotic materials, stronger and lighter than anything naturally occurring. Through selective grafting, farmers grow plants that produce more fruit and that are much more drought and disease resistant than their naturally occurring cousins. Through artistry, sculptors like Michelangelo have chiseled statues that capture the beauty of the human body out of rough blocks of stone.

But all of these things and everything else that we create require the ingredients to *already exist*. Genetic engineers don't create new species out of nothing. They manipulate chemicals and DNA that already exist to conjure up a variation of something that already exists. Chefs don't snap their fingers and spontaneously cover a table in fine food (unless you're watching some TV show). They must take time to properly mix and cook the ingredients.

God on the other hand is not limited by anything and CAN create something literally from NOTHING!

What's That on the Ground?!

After God had delivered Moses and the children of Israel out of Egypt, they had to cross a desert wilderness to get to the Promised Land. Very quickly, the Israelites became hangry and demanded that

Moses provide them with food or they were going to turn back and return to Egypt.

As usual when confronted with a seemingly impossible situation, Moses turned to God and asked for help. Exodus 16:14 (NLT) records how God answered Moses' desperate request:

> When the dew evaporated, a flaky substance as fine as frost blanketed the ground. The Israelites were puzzled when they saw it. "What is it?" they asked each other. They had no idea what it was. And Moses told them, "It is the bread the Lord has given you to eat."

They called this miraculous food *manna*. But even though it was an answer to prayer, there was a catch with it: As soon as the sun arose, the manna evaporated! Even more interesting to me is that if people tried to horde it in their tents, it would become infested with worms! *Yuck!*

To me, it's quite clear that God was wanting the Israelites to trust and rely upon him *daily*. God nourished his followers with his "bread" daily, and I believe that he wants us to come to him through prayer daily, expecting the spiritual and physical nourishment to make it through *that* day and *that* day only.

In the classic Alcoholics Anonymous book *As Bill Sees It*, author Bill W. shares how important it is to have this daily bread:

> Those of us who have come to make regular use of prayer would no more do without it than we would air, food, or sunshine. And when we turn away from meditation and prayer, we deprive our minds and our emotions. As a body can fall without nourishment, so can the soul.

We all need the light of God's reality, the nourishment of his strength.

My prayer for you is that you are beginning to see the depth and power of "Give us this day, our daily bread."

2. Release your pride by choosing to trust God.

Pride has been at the root of many of my problems. If you were to ask me if I'm prideful, a few years ago I would have said, "No way! I don't walk around with my nose in the air, looking down upon people. I don't use fancy words when I speak or brag about my accomplishments. In fact, I feel like I'm always putting myself last in order to serve other people!"

BUT...then...I began to see and understand that my long-held beliefs of "You owe me" and "I don't need you" are actually manifestations of pride!

BANG!

You Don't Need Me

I witnessed this extension of pride first hand in my marriage. For the longest time, if something needed to be fixed or redone at home, I'd gallantly ride in on a stallion and boldly declare, "I'm here! I'll fix this!" as I pushed aside my sweet wife Rhonda.

Then on one key day, I was giving orders to Rhonda, and she'd finally had enough. In a burst of held-back emotions, she revealed, "Jeff, you make me feel like you don't need me!"

BANG!

It felt like my heart stopped. Her words echoed in my ears, and I readied a stinging come back but then closed my mouth. Her words clanged like a bell in my head, and I realized...*she was right!* I was treating—had been treating her for a long time—like I didn't need her. And the truth was and still is: *I need her!*

Pride in the Garden

Pride is the root of many sins and goes all the way back to our ancient ancestors Adam and Eve. You may say, "I thought Adam and Eve were tempted to sin by eating the forbidden fruit in the Garden of Eden?" You are correct!

But if you carefully read the account in Genesis, you'll see that they weren't just tempted to do something that God had told them not to do. Adam and Eve were tempted by the serpent with the idea of being as great and knowledgeable as God. Their willful decision to break God's command was motivated by the serpent's promise that they would become like gods if they ate the forbidden fruit, and the seed of pride was planted within the human race through their disobedience.

Jesus' prayer, "Give us this day our daily bread," encourages us to release our pride and to put our trust, not in our abilities, knowledge, money, or status, but in God's love for us and in the truth that he is greater than anything that could challenge us every day of our lives.

How would your life change if you moved from carrying your daily burdens alone to praying and believing: "God, you've got this! Give me this day, my daily bread."

It's been a game changer for me, and I believe it could be one for you as well!

3. Plant the deeds you want to harvest.

I'm sure you've heard the old phrase, "What goes around, comes around." Did you know that there's a Bible verse that states this? Check out what Galatians 6:7 says:

> Do not be deceived: God cannot be mocked. A man
> reaps what he sows.

Thinking about your own life right now, what do you see growing in the field of your life? Joy? Anger? Peace? Conflict? Faith? Anxiety? You fill in the blanks with whatever you see cropping up in your life, good or bad and everything in between.

The next question I ask—and don't be upset with me for asking this because it's important for your own growth—how many of the things growing in the field of your life did you plant yourself somewhere along the way?

Fire the Gardener!

If upon inspecting your life's field you find a lot of "weeds" and "thorns" growing all over the place, at first, you might be tempted to blame a lot of other people in your life for planting all kinds of undesirable things. And, yes, other people, like family, friends, teachers, coworkers, and so on, can plant unpleasant things in your life.

But I leave you with this deep thought to ponder now and for a long time from now: *Whose field is it?*

Who owns your life? Who lives your life? Who's responsible for tending the field of your life? You might groan, "Me." Yes, *you.*

But there's power here, my friend! I challenge you: If you see things growing in your life that you don't like or want, uproot them and plant something beneficial in their place!

Speaking in a plainer way, if you want to experience kindness in your life, plant kindness in the lives of others. If you want to experience the freedom of forgiveness, forgive others for things that they have done to you. If you want more love, yep, show love to others.

This may seem obvious to most of you when you read this, but I promise you that LIVING the concept of harvesting what you plant in others is not always easy and will lead to PROFOUND and LIFE-CHANGING growth and blessings in your life!

Jesus said it this way in Luke 6:38:

> "Give, and it will be given to you. A good measure, pressed down, shaken together and running over, will be poured into your lap. For with the measure you use, it will be measured to you."

The powerful "secret" here is that you *plant* what you *want to harvest.* Give to others what you want. Treat others as you wish to be treated. I say, "Where you have a need, plant a seed." My friend, plant lots of good seeds out there in your life and watch God give you a harvest that is beyond measure just when you need it the most!

Remember this as you pray: "Give us this day our daily bread."

Chapter 10

How to Receive Forgiveness

"And forgive us our sins"

Imagine being rushed to the hospital while you're in severe pain. A doctor examines you in the ER and recommends immediate surgery. That whirlwind of pain, worry, and uncertainty would be fearful for most people, and you may have already experienced a similar situation in your own life or the life of someone close to you.

That rush to the hospital and emergency surgery happened to my sister a few years ago. She was doubled over from a mysterious pain that seemed to stab her from inside her body. When she finally was examined by a doctor, he discovered that her gallbladder had become inflamed to the point that it could rupture and threaten her life!

She agreed to have it removed, and the procedure went well. In a short time, she was fully recovered and very grateful that the stabbing pains were gone.

And then a different pain arrived in her mailbox.

She began receiving bills from the hospital and notifications from her insurance company. Unfortunately, her health insurance had only paid a percentage of the costs, leaving her with a remainder of around $8,000 to pay on her own. My sister didn't have that kind of money. She was able to work out a payment plan with the doctor but at the cost of $400 a month, which was a tremendous strain on her family.

During the next 5 months, she prayed, asking God to help her with this burdening bill. Then in December of the same year, she retrieved her mail from her mailbox. As she flipped through the envelopes, her heart started racing when she saw a letter from the doctor who performed the gallbladder removal. All kinds of worried thoughts rushed through her head, and she hesitated opening the letter. "What are they charging me for, now?!" she mumbled.

Her curiosity finally won out, and she ripped open the envelope. As her eyes scanned the contents of the letter, she stopped reading and started back at the top to make sure she wasn't missing something. The piece of paper in her hands wasn't another bill; it was a letter stating that the $6,000 remaining on her bill had been forgiven!

Wow! Can you imagine the joy that raced through her as her strangling, financial burden was lifted?

That is how forgiveness feels!

Breaking the House Rules

Have you ever asked God to forgive you, and you felt like he didn't? Or perhaps you've questioned within your mind, "Will God actually forgive me for what I did?"

Back when I was a child, I was responsible for making sure that all the house chores were done by the time that my mom got home from work. I remember this one time I knew I had to take the trash out. I knew that Mom hated for the kitchen trash can to turn into a stinky mountain of overflowing garbage. But on this day, the weather was beautiful, and I saw that my friends were outside playing. I thought, "I've got plenty of time to take out the trash." And I joined my friends in playing games and riding my bike.

Somehow, I lost track of time, and before long, there was my mom's car, coming down the street! I panicked! I rushed back inside and tried to pull the garbage bag out, but it was stuck. As I tugged and tugged at it, the bag finally broke free from the trash can, just as my mom walked inside the kitchen! Caught!

My backside learned an important lesson that day: Take out the trash before Mom gets home!

I tell this story to illustrate sin. I had broken a house rule, and there was a consequence. We've all had similar experiences growing up of getting in trouble at home, at school, at church, at a store, in the car, and so on. And the consequences that we received varied depending upon who was disciplining us and how they judged the severity of the offense. We were grounded, spanked, or scolded.

Looking at sin, there is always a price to pay, even when it looks like people have gotten away with it. God sees all; nothing can be hidden from him.

The good news I wish to share with you is that Jesus paid the tremendous price for our sins and has granted us the freedom to openly ask the Father to forgive us for our sins.

You may say, "Okay, Jeff, but how do I receive God's forgiveness?" Let me step you through three concepts that will help you receive God's forgiveness.

1. I must change my perspective of how God thinks of me.

Have you ever met someone who you felt didn't like you? How about a pastor? It may seem strange to you that another pastor doesn't like me—after all, aren't pastors supposed to like everybody? Well, for whatever reason, this particular pastor just doesn't like me. I've tried to extend kindness to him, spoken to him with an open mind, and prayed for him. But he still doesn't like me.

You probably have people in your family or at work who, despite every attempt by you to extend an olive branch of peace, just don't care for you. It's frustrating and perplexing at the same time!

So, have you ever stopped to think about what God thinks about you? In your mind, does God the Father have his arm reared back ready to throw down a lightning bolt on you?

The best way I can think to show you how God thinks about you is to let the Bible speak up on this subject. And does it speak! Let's just take 2 verses from the book of John and ponder God's thoughts about us:

> For God so loved the world that he gave his one and
> only Son, that whoever believes in him shall not perish
> but have eternal life. For God did not send his Son into
> the world to condemn the world, but to save the world
> through him.

To make these extraordinary verses more personal, read back through them one more time and replace the word "world" with *your* name!

Wow! That's what God thinks about you, my friend! He loves you so much that he gave his life for you! He wants to forgive you for your sins.

2. I must accept that Jesus paid for my forgiveness.

In my family, we grew up with the thinking that if something sounds too good to be true, it probably is. When my sister received the letter in the mail informing her that her medical bill had been forgiven, she was skeptical at first. She couldn't believe or accept the debt forgiveness being extended to her.

So, she called her doctor's office, inquiring about the unusual letter. Had there been some kind of back office mistake? To her delighted surprise, she learned that at the end of each year, the doctor chose some outstanding accounts to forgive, and hers had been selected. There was no mistake!

In essence, the doctor paid for my sister's substantial medical bill by forgiving it.

Our sin—all our sins lumped together—is like an unfathomably large debt that we cannot pay. Payment required the death of a sinless sacrifice, yet none of us could even offer our death as payment to God since we are not sinless.

Romans 6:23 (TLB) declares, "For the wages of sin is death, but the free gift of God is eternal life through Jesus Christ our Lord."

There needed to be a savior for humanity, sinless in purity, and willing to lay down his life. Jesus is that person, the only one in the whole universe who was qualified to be the ultimate sacrifice for the redemption of our lives. Jesus paid the bill that was owed to God because of our sins.

Even as Jesus endured the unending agony of torture on the cross, he blessed the very people that were torturing him and pleaded with the Father to have mercy on them. "Father, forgive them," Jesus said, as recorded in Luke 23:33, "for they do not know what they are doing."

For us today, I believe that Jesus was saying in that plea, "Father, let all of their sins be applied to me. Forgive them. I'm paying for their forgiveness."

With his head bowing, Jesus finally uttered the words from the cross, "It is finished," and so completed his willing sacrifice for our salvation.

We should rejoice that our debt of sin has been paid! The cost was far more than any of us could ever pay, but even more earth-shaking is that Jesus now offers us this forgiveness as a FREE gift to anyone who will accept it!

1 John 1:9 (NCV) says that:

> If we confess our sins, he will forgive our sins, because
> we can trust God to do what is right. He will cleanse us
> from all the wrongs we have done.

If you aren't currently a follower of Christ, I strongly encourage you to surrender your life to Christ Jesus and to receive his free gift of salvation and forgiveness for your sins. If you would like to start your journey following Jesus, here's a short prayer to help you get started. You can pray this out loud or silently to yourself.

> **Dear Jesus, I know that I am a sinner. I ask for your forgiveness. I believe that you died for my sins. I trust and follow you as my Lord and Savior. Please help me turn away from sin and help me to do your will. In Jesus' name, Amen!**

3. I must walk in the power of God's forgiveness.

The life of Jesus did not end on the cross or in the tomb that he was buried in. Unlike any of the greatest kings, queens, philosophers, theologians, inventors, writers, artists, musicians, scientists, and religious leaders throughout time, Jesus is the ONLY one to have resurrected HIMSELF from the dead! The only one!

The apostle Paul made it clear that Jesus' resurrection is God's seal of approval on all that Jesus said and claimed about himself. You've probably heard the saying "the proof is in the pudding." The proof that Jesus is the Son of God and that he spoke the truth is in his resurrection.

When some of the women that followed Jesus visited his burial site after the crucifixion, they were stunned to find that the large stone used to seal the tomb had been ripped aside. And as recorded in Matthew 25:5-6, an angel appeared to them saying:

> "Do not be afraid, for I know that you are looking for
> Jesus, who was crucified. He is not here; he has risen,
> just as he said. Come and see the place where he lay."

Sin kills something inside of you and ultimately wishes to make your life a tomb of dead dreams, lifeless living, and hopeless dread. The physical grave was meant to confine Jesus...but it couldn't! In addition to closing off the entrance to the tomb with a massive stone, the Romans posted soldiers in front of it so that Jesus' disciples couldn't "steal" his body.

But when Jesus arose from the dead on the third day, the Bible records that the soldiers fell flat like dead men, terrified by the power of God emanating from that place.

But to me, even more spectacular than all of the supernatural forces at work in regenerating Jesus' body is God's love on display for all of the world to see in this scene! My friend, it is God's love that raised Jesus, and it is God's love that breathes new life into our lives! And it is God's love that has made a place for us to go once we die.

Listen to how 1 Corinthians 15:54-57 (NLT) describes what awaits those who follow Jesus after they pass:

> Then, when our dying bodies have been transformed into bodies that will never die, the Scripture will be fulfilled: "Death is swallowed up in victory. O death, where is your victory? O death, where is your sting?" For sin is the sting that results in death...But thank God! He gives us victory over sin and death through our Lord Jesus Christ.

Death has lost its sting because God has forgiven our sins. My friend, you don't have to be afraid of death if you are a follower of Christ because God has already taken the sting out of it.

The Sting of Death

I'm reminded of a story about a father who was riding in a car with his children. They were driving along, looking at the beautiful scenery of the great Smoky Mountains. With the windows down, they breathed in the fresh mountain air.

Suddenly, a bee flew into the car.

The father's little daughter in the backseat started panicking. She was highly allergic to bee stings. As the bee buzzed into the back of the car, the father kept one hand on the steering wheel and with the other hand, slammed the bee upward, trapping it against the roof of the car.

The father winced as the bee stung him, but then he relaxed. He released the bee, much to his little girl's terror.

As the bee buzzed around the car again, the little girl cried, "Daddy! It's going to sting me!"

In a soothing voice, the father replied, "Don't worry, baby girl. I have the stinger in my hand. The bee may be flying around, but he doesn't have the ability to sting you anymore."

This is a picture of what Jesus did for us. He took the sting out of death by dying for us and then rising from the dead. By living in the power of God's forgiveness, the fear of death—it's stinger—is removed.

If you are a follower of Christ, you don't have to fear death anymore! You have a hope and a promise that cannot be broken by any power! Walk in the power of God's forgiveness.

Just like my sister pulls out the letter forgiving her medical bill from time to time to remind her about what God can do, whenever you feel guilty about your past sins which you've already confessed to God, just pull out God's letter to you, the Bible, and read it. Let it refresh within you the resurrection power of Jesus. Let it remind you that your sins have been paid in full!

Father, forgive my sins.

Chapter 11

The Prayer of Release

"As we forgive those who sin against us"

There are problems, and then there are PROBLEMS. In this life, we are hit by money problems, health problems, car problems, house problems, and more. But one problem that I believe towers above the rest is relationship problems. Can I get an *amen*?!

I have a question for you: If your relationships were in order—in other words, *people ain't buggin' the daylights out of ya*—how much happier would you be every day?

Conflict with others can cause us to feel hurt, disappointed, discouraged, angry, guilty, fearful, and on and on. And I'm *not* saying that you'll be able to completely free yourself from relationship issues in this world. Even Jesus had to endure disagreements and hurt feelings among his disciples, who were literally hanging out 24/7 with the Prince of Peace.

However, Jesus gives us the secret to having internal happiness and peace despite people problems, and I promise you, it's NOT how your human body and mind want to react.

The Good, the Bad, and the Jealous

In the book of Genesis, Joseph started off in life as the youngest son to Jacob, a man who already had a bunch of sons from different wives. Now, Jacob was the grandson of Abraham, the very person who God had made a covenant with to mightily bless him and his descendants above any other family in the world. But looking at young Joseph's life, that blessing didn't seem to bring much peace to their family.

Joseph's 10 brothers seem to always be looking for a fight, either with each other or with other people from surrounding tribes. To make matters worse, God gave Joseph dreams about how one day, *he* would be put in charge of his older brothers.

Well, you can imagine how well that went over with his 10 brothers. Behind the scenes, they were angry! They grumbled and complained to each other about this little, haughty pip-squeak.

Worse still, their father Jacob made a beautiful coat of many colors and gave it to Joseph, the youngest child! In their culture, the best blessings were to go to the oldest son first and then trickle down the line of children, much like hand-me-downs from older children to younger children today.

Joseph's brothers were so infuriated by his special treatment that they plotted to kill him. How's that for family unity?! Talk about relationship problems!

If you don't know what happened next, the brothers threw Joseph in a pit, and after an intense fight over what to do with him, Joseph's brothers sold him to slave traders going to Egypt. The brothers then shredded Joseph's precious coat, stained it with blood, and it presented it to their father, claiming that a wild animal had killed Joseph.

Lies, deception, jealousy, and hatred marked how these brothers dealt with their relationship problem. In your life, you may have felt similar emotions and wanted to do things that you'd feel embarrassed to admit to get even with someone who's wronged you. Trust me, I'm not judging you; I, too, have wanted to lash out at people, and to my regret, I have used words to hurt the very people I love and respect.

We all face relationship situations over and over throughout life; it's part of being human. But there is hope. There is a better way to react, and both Joseph and Jesus show us the way.

From Slavery to Prison

The slave traders sold Joseph to an Egyptian named Potiphar. I'm sure Joseph was very depressed at first to have been torn away from his family and homeland, but eventually Joseph moved forward and distinguished himself as a brilliant leader, so much so that he was put in charge of the household and business of the very man who had purchased him.

Just as life was going great for Joseph, disaster struck! Potiphar's wife tried to seduce Joseph, and when he refused her advances, she claimed that he had attempted to seduce her!

In a flash, Joseph was thrown in prison. Over the next 10 years in a holding cell, Joseph had plenty of opportunities to boil in anger and resentment over his mistreatment. He could've plotted his revenge against Potiphar and his wife. He could've sunk into despair and lost the will to live. But he put his trust in God, the very one who still gave him dreams, and not before long, Joseph won the trust of his jailors and ascended to be chief representative of the prisoners! People just can't keep this guy down!

Joseph may have lost everything around him, but he never lost faith in God.

From Prison to Palace

Word spread of Joseph's ability to interpret dreams, and when the Pharaoh of Egypt was troubled by a nightmare that refused to leave his mind, Joseph was called up out of the prison and forced to appear before the mighty king.

As Pharaoh retold his perplexing dream of 7 healthy cows being devoured by 7 zombie-like cows rising out of the Nile River, God instantly gave Joseph the interpretation: For 7 years, Egypt would be blessed with abundant crops, but in the following 7 years, Egypt would be cursed with famine.

Pharaoh was so overwhelmed with relief from the mysterious dream and amazed at the 14-year prediction that he promoted Joseph—who was not even an Egyptian—to second in command over Egypt and made him the chief project manager over preparing the country for the impending famine.

Joseph literally went from prison to palace in one day thanks to God's blessing! But I believe that it was Joseph's willingness to forgive and move on with his life in the face of all the ill-treatment by others that gave God a willing person to work through.

Today, we can learn from the life of Joseph 3 important steps that will help us forgive others.

1. Remember how much God has forgiven you.

In Genesis 39:21 (NLT), we read that, "The Lord was with Joseph in the prison and showed him his faithful love." Joseph may have been in a physical, stinking prison, but he was spiritually free. He no longer had fine clothes, delicious food, or a comfortable bed to sleep in, but he had God's forgiveness and favor.

I'm sure that Joseph had lots of time to think about his life while in prison. He may have thought back about how he had bragged to his parents that one day he would rule over his brothers just like his dreams had shown him. He may have asked God to forgive him for being boastful and prideful. But I'm 100% certain that this time of reflection in Joseph's life was the start of something great for him. I believe that he chose to forgive others like the way God had forgiven him.

And if you think that last line sounded similar to part of Jesus' prayer, you're right! Jesus teaches us in Matthew 6:12 (NLT):

> "Forgive us our sins, as we have forgiven those who sin against us."

Jesus is crystal clear here that we need to forgive others for the trespasses they've committed against us and that we need to receive God's forgiveness for our own sins. It's just like the concept I mentioned earlier in the book that we harvest what we plant. If we want God to extend forgiveness to us, why should we refuse to forgive those who hurt us?

I'm not saying that forgiving other people is easy; sometimes it is; many times, it's not. But nothing worthwhile is easy. Climbing a mountain isn't easy, but if you've done it, you know that sheer overwhelming joy of the accomplishment. Losing weight and getting into shape, if you're not, isn't easy, but once you've achieved it, a joy that is hard to describe fills you. If you've labored for a long time on a project at home or work, you know the feeling of satisfaction and excitement you get when you step back and admire all of the hard work you did.

Forgiveness is a conscious choice we must make. Sometimes it will be easy; sometimes it will take time and a lot of effort to forgive. But ultimately the choice is ours, which leads me to the next step.

2. Release the people who hurt you.

I confess to you that this one is a challenge for me and might be for you as well. But I have witnessed over and over in my life and the life of others that this step is one of the greatest roads to FREEDOM!

When Joseph's wife bore his first son, he named him *Manasseh*, saying, "God has made me forget all my troubles." Joseph's heart was at peace. He had released his brothers, Potiphar, Potiphar's wife, and all others from the wrongs they had committed against him.

I believe that Joseph still remembered the unfortunate scenes that had altered his life, but having forgiven the people responsible, these events no longer held him prisoner. He had released the guilty people, and in so doing, he had found freedom himself.

Right now, you might say, "Jeff, that's all well and good about forgiving people, but you don't know what this person did to me. Even if I wanted to forgive them, I don't know where to begin or how to do it."

I hear you! Let me help you get started on your road to forgiveness.

Three Ways to Release People Who Have Hurt You

a. Begin by sharing about what happened to you with a person you trust.

Holding on to hurts, grudges, and unforgiveness will eat you up, inside out. People can actually have stomach issues not because of the foods they're eating but because of lingering unforgiveness and the negative emotions that arise from it.

Revealing my hurt is the beginning of healing my hurt. If this section is stirring up memories and emotions from your past, I encourage you to seek out a trusted friend, pastor, or counselor to talk to. One of the greatest gifts I've ever given myself was the gift of going to a counselor. My counselor helped me work through traumatic events from my past which I didn't even realize were causing me pain in the present.

b. Let go of the desire to get even.

It's very human to want to hit someone back who's hit you. But just as Jesus demonstrated when he was beaten by Roman soldiers and forgave them and by the apostle Paul, who was whipped severely, also by a Roman soldier, and forgave them, God wants us to forgive each other.

Though my arguments with my wife Rhonda have been nothing like the injuries Jesus and Paul received to their skin, both of us inflicted deep wounds into each other's heart throughout our marriage. Some of these unseen wounds festered between us for years, causing division between us. But praise God, we both learned to forgive each other and let go of the desire to get even.

I've found that resentment steals contentment.

When we choose to hold on to our hurts from the past, we end up cheating ourselves from the love and freedom we could experience if we were to forgive and let go.

Learn to let go. The sooner you let go and forgive, the sooner you can move on with your life.

c. Change the channel.

So how do we handle thoughts of past hurts that seem to erupt like a volcano out of nowhere and trouble us even after we've forgiven and let go of trying to get even?

You have to change the channel of your mind and let the thoughts drift away like clouds floating out of sight. Colossians 3:13 (NLT) instructs us to:

Make allowances for each other's faults, and forgive anyone who offends you. Remember, the Lord forgave you, so you must forgive others.

When old thoughts resurface, let them be a trigger for you to remember what God has done for you. Let it remind you that he loves you with an endless love and forgives you for your mistakes. Remember what God has done for you instead of what someone has done to you.

3. Realize that God is at work even in the bad times.

A shocking truth about life is that even when it looks like all hell has exploded in a firestorm as far as you can see, God is *nearer* to you than the chaos raging around you. God is with you.

Joseph's life was filled with promotion, then tremendous setback and suffering. Yet, God was with him through it all, and Joseph knew that, even when he felt abandoned. God was with him, protected him, blessed him, and eventually placed him in charge of the economy and food production of the most powerful nation in the region!

And at this point in Joseph's life, God gave him a very ironic gift. Because of the 7-year famine that ravaged the world at the time, people from all over heard word that Egypt had food and traveled great distances to exchange their gold, silver, spices, fine clothing, *anything* of value that they had for food from Egypt's full storehouses.

The Tables Are Turned

As Joseph observed the crowds of people from all over the region who had traveled to Egypt to buy food, he was stunned when he recognized his brothers among the masses! There they were; the ones who had thrown him in the pit as a young man! Now he could have the last laugh; now he could get even and take away everything they owned and then let them and their families starve...

...But no.

That was not how Joseph reacted at all!

Instead of taking revenge on his brothers, Joseph wept seeing them and made a plan to reunite his family! But first, he met with them privately, concealing his identity, and set up tests for his brothers to see if they'd changed.

After multiple visits to Egypt from them, Joseph finally saw that his brothers had matured and developed a love for each other. Unable to keep up his disguise any longer, Joseph revealed his identity to his brothers. The shock on their faces must've been extraordinary!

The brothers were horrified, fearing that Joseph would now exact judgment on them for their deeds, but in one of the most beautiful moments of forgiveness and reconciliation ever recorded, Joseph opened his arms to them and hugged them as brothers reunited. As written in Genesis 45:5,8, he said to them:

> "Do not be distressed and do not be angry with your-
> selves for selling me here, because it was to save lives
> that God sent me ahead of you...It was not you who
> sent me here, but God."

Joseph's response grabs my heart. He could've viciously lashed out at his brothers for what they did to him—and from a human perspective, I'd say he had every right to—but instead, Joseph turns the whole situation around and forgives them and gives glory to God. He reminds us that we can only see a little sliver of reality, but God sees the big picture.

Only God can take something rottenly awful and turn it into a far-reaching blessing. My friend, your past hurt is not bigger than God's plan for your life.

"Forgive my sins, as I forgive those who have sinned against me."

Chapter 12

The Prayer of Deliverance

"Lead us not into temptation, but deliver us from evil"

The very word *temptation* conjures up all kinds of images in our minds. You might think about delicious, high-calorie desserts or attractive models. You might see mountains of hundred-dollar bills or sexy sports cars. The things that can tempt us are literally endless, and each day, advertisers dream up bigger and more outrageous temptations to try to get us to purchase their products or services.

And let me clear up something here. Temptation is *not* sin. Jesus was tempted by Satan but did not give in and did not sin. Temptation is a vehicle that drives up to you and opens the door and says, "Hey! Hop in! I'll take ya' to the good times!" If we hop in and then ride along to its destination, THEN we are sinning.

Sin is one of the chief weapons the devil uses against us to try to hold us back from becoming the victorious person God wants us to be. Satan learned all the way back in the Garden of Eden that humans can be easily led astray by disguising the ugly and lethal end results of sin in a tempting packaging. It worked on our ancient grandparents Adam and

Eve, and Satan has used this same technique over and over for countless generations since then to all peoples everywhere. Temptation and sin are literally universal problems that all people experience and have to deal with.

BUT...and it's imperative that you get this into your mind and heart...though the devil can set up all kinds of temptations for you, he CANNOT make you sin. Like other decisions I've talked about in this book, to sin or not to sin is always your choice.

You might ask, "Where do these temptations come from? And how can I recognize them?"

Let's look at the BIG 3.

The BIG 3

In the Bible, 1 John 2:16 (KJV) gives us 3 categories of temptations to watch out for:

> For all that is in the world, the lust of the flesh, and the
> lust of the eyes, and the pride of life, is not of the Father,
> but is of the world.

1. The Lust of the Flesh

The *lust of the flesh* is related to human appetites and cravings. These are lower-level, base instincts and desires, which I believe that God built into our DNA for the preservation of our species in a dangerous world. However, just as God elevated humans above all the rest of the animals on this planet, we are to reign these desires in and only give them place in the boundaries that God has defined for us in the Bible.

You may say, "Well, wait a minute...If God put these instincts within us, what's wrong with just following them?" My answer is that we are NOT animals. We may share biology with the animals of this world, but God distinguished us from them by giving us a soul and higher reasoning when he breathed his Spirit into Adam.

Unlike animals, we normally do not go around ripping food out of other people's hands to then smash it into our faces. In fact, if we saw someone doing that as they walked down the street, we'd probably be alarmed because we'd instantly know that something was wrong.

We also don't normally gorge ourselves on food until we are ready to vomit, unless we're in some kind of hotdog-eating contest! (And when the contest is over, stay away from the contestants!) We wear clothes for modesty, also begun with Adam and Eve, and we don't have sex with every person we meet in the street like some dog in heat! Heaven help us!

Anthropologists have studied tribes who have lived in isolated places all over the world, and in every instance, these tribes have many rules that govern what their people can and cannot do. We are not animals.

The lusts of the flesh will appeal to deep desires, but we must keep them in check or they will check us out.

2. The Lust of the Eyes

Have you ever seen a piece of jewelry sparkling in a store window that you found yourself going back to look at over and over? You were mesmerized by its brilliance and couldn't seem to take your eyes away from it? How about a brand-new, decked-out, glossy new muscle car or truck or SUV? Maybe you took a lunch break to visit a dealership and before you knew it, found yourself taking a test drive—or maybe even driving your new purchase back to work!

I know people who have done these things, and they were captured by the lust of their eyes. They saw something, and it connected with something inside of them, and they went back to look again, and again, until they finally gave in.

Now, buying jewelry or vehicles or clothes or electronics or any endless number of "gotta-have" things for sale in our world, is not necessarily a sin, but if you're putting yourself into financial bondage because you HAVE TO HAVE something, this should be a big warning sign to you! In fact, any time that you feel like you *have to have* something, you should question yourself with, "Do I really need this?"

You need to be aware that temptations in the lust-of-the-eyes category have a very strong pull over us. Once we see something, and we want it, it can be an all-out fight *within ourselves* to say "No!"

And I'm not just talking about food and material things here. I'm also talking about being sexually attracted to people you're around and trying to build up a relationship with someone to "see where it goes." If you're single, you gotta slow down and get to know the person without sex. If you're married, you gotta axe these thoughts down and burn them, or you could be headed for adultery, divorce, and hell on earth!

The lust of the eyes is real, strong, and experienced by everybody, probably every day in some way. But there is hope! We are not alone. God can help us win these daily battles! Now you have an even greater understanding of why we should pray: "Lead me not into temptation, but deliver me from evil."

3. The Pride of Life

If I asked you what Satan's original sin was, how would you answer? If you responded with "pride," you got it!

At one time, Satan was a beautiful angel named Lucifer, who was skilled with words and music. But he began to think that he was greater than God, his Creator, and wanted to exalt himself over God. The Bible doesn't share many details about what happened, but what it does share is shocking. Lucifer became so filled with pride that he became a corrupted creature who persuaded a third of the angels in heaven to fight on his side against the Father.

Now, you take an infinitely-powered God versus a created being with limited power and any child can tell you who would win. But Lucifer was so blinded by his own pride and vanity that he actually believed he'd win.

And he lost. Spectacularly!

God instantly flung him and his followers out of heaven in a flaming ball of ruin and cursed them forever! Jesus even reported to his disciples in Luke 10:18 that he saw Satan fall like lightning from heaven. *Boom!*

But guess what: We are tempted with the pride of life as well.

If you've ever started feeling like you're better or superior to someone else, yep, that's the pride of life starting to sneak into your thinking. If you feel like you've got so much success that nothing could ever happen to you, watch out! You have no clue what could be just around the corner of your life. If you think, "My money will rescue me; I don't need God's help," beware! Money can buy things, yes; but not everything. Trust me, I've visited plenty of wealthy people in hospitals who would've given everything to get better, but their money was worthless in the end.

I'm not telling you to not be "proud" of your child or "proud" of completing a challenging project or "proud" of your service for our country or "proud" of your spouse for putting up with you for years.

I'm talking about the pride of life which says, "I'm better than anyone, and I don't need God!" The pride of life sneaks in, twists your thinking, convinces you of your superiority, and distances you from God.

Do you remember from history the Nazi party of Germany? One of their core teachings was that the "Aryan race" (whatever that is) was superior to all other races and ethnicities in the world. THAT thinking is the pride of life. And what resulted from this pride? The horrific death of millions of innocent people and the destruction of Germany at the end of World War II!

The pride of life is a temptation that ultimately brings destruction to its believer. Stay away from this, my friend!

The Big 3 types of temptations are all around us and try to grab our attention every day. It's spiritual warfare, with unseen attacks and traps set for us by Satan. But we should not be afraid. If you are a Christ follower, God is on your side and available to help. Suddenly Jesus' words, "lead us not into temptation, but deliver us from evil," are very, very important and relevant to our daily lives!

Marco!

I was on a mission trip to Honduras with some people from our church. We had worked all day in the heat, ridden for miles in a hot van back to our not-so deluxe hotel. But there was a pool at the hotel, and all I could think of at the end of the day was to jump into its cool water!

Once back at my room, I changed into a swimsuit and headed to the pool area with some of our team. Upon seeing the pool, I was kind of disappointed; it looked small. But it didn't matter; I would soon be enjoying its refreshing water.

As I walked by some of our team members who were standing by the pool, I suddenly had a flash of inspiration: I'd push one of them into the pool! "That'll be funny," I thought. "We'll all have a laugh."

And so...I did it!

I pushed in the closest team member, and *whoosh*, a scream followed along with a huge splash of water and laughs from other team members standing around the pool. I laughed, too, thinking this was a fun practical joke.

But when the girl resurfaced and wiped the water off her face, she gave me a stern look and said, "Pastor Jeff, you had the devil on one shoulder and an angel on the other. You must've listened to the devil!"

I thought for a moment and responded, "I don't think the angel showed up!"

She burst out laughing, and we all had a great laugh at this.

There is so much truth to what she said. There is always the presence of good and evil with us daily. But again, there is hope!

To help you defeat the lust of the flesh, the lust of the eyes, and the pride of life, I'd like to share with you some practical techniques that will help you escape temptations when they come calling.

1. Identify what you are vulnerable to.

Let's face it; we're all vulnerable to things. Jesus himself was tempted by Satan for his whole life. From hunger, to sexual desire, to desire for power, Jesus had temptation after temptation hurled at him. Even on the cross, people—probably spurred on by Satan—tempted him to come down off the cross to stop God's plan of redemption. But Jesus found his strength to resist all of the temptations through prayer and Scripture.

In 1 Corinthians 10:13 (NLT), Paul writes:

The temptations in your life are no different from what others experience. And God is faithful. He will not allow the temptation to be more than you can stand. When you are tempted, he will show you a way out so that you can endure.

Four key takeaways from this passage are:

- Every temptation you face has been faced and is being faced by other people as well. You are not alone with these struggles.

- God is faithful. God does not abandon you just because you are being tempted. He is there to help you choose not to give in and to offer you forgiveness if you fail.

- God will never allow you to be tempted beyond what you can handle. Sometimes when I am being tempted, I will say, "God, you have more faith in me than I have in myself right now."

- God will always show you how to remove yourself from the temptation.

I want to follow up this verse with 4 questions for you to ask yourself to help you identify your vulnerability.

- *When* am I most tempted?
- *Where* am I most tempted?
- *Who* is with me when I'm most tempted?
- *How* do I feel right *before* I'm tempted?

Jesus is clear about the number one defense we have against temptation. Listen to his words in Matthew 26:41:

"Watch and pray so that you will not fall into temptation. The spirit is willing, but the flesh is weak."

Through the years, I've had many people talk to me about a sin in their life that took them farther than they ever wanted to go, kept them longer than they wanted to stay, and cost them more than they wanted to pay. According to them, it was like they were unaware of what was happening because they were subtly being led into a trap, a trap which they did not escape.

When we pray regularly, our minds are attuned more to the things of God, and I can tell you from experience that when one of these traps appears, you instantly see it for what it is and run the other way!

Lead me not into temptation, God!

2. Make plans ahead of time to avoid temptation.

Have you ever heard this saying: "If you don't want to get stung, stay away from the bees!" I always chuckle when I hear this one, but there is so much truth contained in those words. The Bible says it this way in Proverbs 4:26 (TEV):

Plan carefully what you do, and whatever you do will turn out right.

Most people never think about creating a plan ahead of time of what they would do if they were tempted. I believe that most people would say, "Aw, I'll figure out something when the time comes." The problem is that by the time we are tempted, we're already being pulled in like a fish on a reel. It would've been so much better to have recognized the bait and seen the hook and then swam away as fast as we could instead of winding up on a dinner plate!

Dating

I was a student pastor for 5 ½ years before I became a lead pastor. Working with teenagers, they'd constantly ask me for advice on how to handle dating, especially the tempting situations that can arise out of being alone with your date.

I'd offer them this advice: Make a plan ahead of time of where you are going and how far you are physically going to go with each other and stick to the plan! Either you'll follow the plan or go with your glands!

Traveling

Personally, I have found my greatest time of temptation to be when I travel overnight and have to stay in a hotel alone. I'm tempted to watch things on TV that are inappropriate, so early on, I decided that I'd make a plan to combat these temptations.

First, I try not to travel alone. If I can bring Rhonda, a staff member, or a close friend, I do! My relationship with Rhonda, my children, my church, and God are worth far more to me than having to pay some small expenses for a person to accompany me.

Second, if I have to travel alone, I don't turn the TV on at all. I may go to a restaurant or work out in the hotel gym if there is one. I also bring a couple of books to choose from to read and may do so in the lobby. When I get sleepy, I return to my room and go to bed. Simple. Done.

Third, the best way to reduce my temptations significantly is to pray the Lord's Prayer daily. When I get to "lead me not into temptation but deliver me from evil," I say, "God, you know what I can handle, so please lead me away from the temptation that is stronger than me and keep those strong temptations away from me."

3. Guard your heart.

Temptation takes root inside of you. The longer you dwell on thinking about something or keep returning to it, its seed will eventually make its way down into your heart and sprout. Soon this sapling grows into your mind and begins to tell your emotions how great it would be to have the thing you're thinking about. By the time this growing vine has wrapped around your heart, mind, and emotions, you begin to take action to fulfill the temptation.

But, if you guard your heart to begin with, you can prevent the seed of temptation from taking root within your mind. And if you do discover "weeds" growing up inside your heart and mind, you can pluck them out before they take over.

We guard our heart by paying close attention to what we spend time thinking on, particularly any fantasies you whisk yourself away on.

Consider David's Psalm 19:14 (NLT):

> May the words of my mouth and the meditation of my heart be pleasing to you, O Lord, my rock and my redeemer.

If we think it and feel it, chances are high that we'll act on it.

The great theologian Martin Luther said it this way: "You cannot keep birds from flying over your head, but you can keep them from building a nest in your hair."

OUCH!

When I was about 8 years old, my brother was about to cut our neighbor's yard. For some reason, he thought he should lower the height of the mower *while the lawnmower was on!*

As my brother started reaching under the mower, I ran over and shut the mower off.

You'd think he would've been grateful to me for sparing him tremendous pain, but instead, he was furious with me, yelling at me to leave him alone and let him do what he wanted. Angrily, he cranked the mower back up and jabbed his hand under the mower deck to adjust the height.

Before I could react, there was a horrible chopping sound followed by my brother's intense scream. The mower blade had cut his finger almost off!

I still cringe remembering that scene, my brother in agony, the blood, the fear. But this moment in my life reminds me a lot of what I've observed in so many people's lives around me as they gave in to temptation. It hurt me to watch them as their relationships or physical bodies or finances fell apart, all because of choosing to follow their temptations.

And worse than it hurt me seeing these things, it hurt their families even more. I so wished that they would've chosen differently, and I pray that you will choose differently in your life.

4. Pray for deliverance daily.

Even before the big tech revolution of today, people have been faced with all kinds of evil. Now, it's literally everywhere, seeking you out on your phone, in apps, on your computer, and whatever other devices connect to the internet.

It may seem like it's almost impossible to resist the temptations flying at us, but as Christ followers, we have a tremendous advantage. Jesus is with us, and he understands what we face. Listen to how Hebrews 4:14-16 (NLT) describes Jesus:

> So then, since we have a great High Priest who has entered heaven, Jesus the Son of God, let us hold firmly to what we believe. This High Priest of ours understands our weaknesses, for he faced all of the same testings we do, yet he did not sin. So let us come boldly to the throne of our gracious God. There we will receive his mercy, and we will find grace to help us when we need it most.

Jesus understands our weaknesses and gives charge to the Holy Spirit to help us defeat temptation. By going to God's throne in prayer daily, we receive the gift of mercy. What is mercy? Mercy is NOT getting what we deserve if we sin. I thank God for his mercy, because without it, where would we be?!

Through prayer, we also receive another gift from God: grace. Sometimes people interchange mercy and grace, but they are not the same thing. God's grace is when he gives you something you don't deserve. Salvation is the ultimate example of grace because none of us deserve an eternity in heaven, and yet, God extends his grace to us when we accept Jesus as our savior.

And grace doesn't stop with salvation. God can bless us with grace in many, many ways in our everyday lives. In fact, every time he answers a prayer of yours, you could see it as God's grace being showered upon you.

There's so much to gain by praying daily, why wouldn't you do it? What are you waiting for?

Praying the Perfect Prayer

My friend, I challenge you to pray the Lord's Prayer every day and watch how God changes your life. I recommend that you pray this prayer once a day for a month with the helping statements beside.

The Perfect Prayer

Our Father, who is in heaven–Thank you, God, for loving me.

Hallowed be your name–I praise you, God, for who you are, what you have done, and what you can do.

Your kingdom come, your will be done, on earth as it is in heaven–Have your way, God, in my life.

Give us this day, our daily bread–Give me what I need for today.

And forgive our sins–Father, forgive me.

As we forgive those who have sinned against us–Help me to forgive others even when it's difficult to do so.

And lead us not into temptation but deliver us from evil–Help me to see temptations for what they are and help me to run away from them.

My friend, may you pray this perfect prayer with understanding every day! May its words and structure help you create your own special prayers and help you grow closer in your relationship with God! May you find hope and strength in praying its words and the courage to live a victorious and successful life!

God bless you!